PAUSE

FOR -----------------

THOUGHT

WATKINS

Sharing Wisdom Since
1893

PAUSE FOR THOUGHT

First published in the UK and USA in 2016 by Watkins, an imprint of Watkins Media Limited
19 Cecil Court
London WC2N 4EZ

enquiries@watkinspublishing.com

By arrangement with the BBC
The BBC logo is a trade mark of the British Broadcasting Corporation and is used under licence.
BBC logo copyright © BBC 2005
Radio 2 logo copyright © Radio 2 2005

Publisher: Jo Lal
Development Editor: Fiona Robertson
Editor: Rebecca Shepherd
Design and Picture Research: Francesca Corsini
Production: Uzma Taj

TBI Media Project Co-ordinator: Harad Smith

A CIP record for this book is available from the British Library

ISBN: 978-1-78028-980-9

10 9 8 7 6 5 4 3 2 1

Colour reproduction by XY Digital
Printed in Bosnia and Herzegovina

Publisher's Note: Scripts may not be exactly as broadcast, but are always substantively so.

www.watkinspublishing.com

PHOTOGRAPHIC ACKNOWLEDGEMENTS

The publisher would like to thank the following individuals and websites for permission to reproduce their material. Any errors or omissions are entirely unintentional and the publishers will, if informed, make amendments in future editions of this book: Page 8 NASA/Unsplash; 12 Atlas Green/Unsplash; 31 (clockwise from top left) Janice Nice, Joanna Wallace, Rebecca Lawrence, Robin Greenwell, Andrew Oliver, Thomas Leleux; 40 Leon Seierlein/Unsplash; 46-7 Robin Röcker/Unsplash; 51 Christopher Sardegna/Unsplash; 78 Artem Verbo/Unsplash; 88 Patrick Hendry/Unsplash; 93 Ezra Jeffrey/Unsplash; 103 (clockwise from top left) Gary Styles, Andrew Oakes, Jayne Jones, Helen Shallow, Oliver Websdell, Carol Thomas; 116-17 Désirée Fawn/Unsplash; 140 Roxane Clediere/Unsplash; 151 (clockwise from top left) Ellie Edwards, Steve Hopton, Rachel Pollard, Ewa Mackeonis, Jeff Smith, Karen Dutton; 158 Jeremy Cai/Unsplash; 160 Alex Holt/Unsplash; 168 Jeff Sheldon/Unsplash. All other images Shutterstock.com.

CONTENTS

FOREWORD BY CHRIS EVANS

I love Pause *for* Thought. *I always look forward to hearing who has to say what. All of our contributors are brilliant, without exception, each bringing their unique mixture of character, style, wisdom and experience on to the airwaves. As the world continues to speed up at an exponential rate, it is more important than ever before to take a beat, take a breath and take a moment to consider why we're doing what we're doing and what we might be doing better.*

I am spoilt because I get to hear the Pause for Thoughts *on the* Radio 2 Breakfast Show *first hand, but even when I'm not in the studio I seem to have evolved a habit of seeking them out elsewhere, on other programmes on the network. What's important is important. And sometimes we need a reminder of what those important things might be. That's what* Pause For Thought *never fails to do. Long live those who bother to pause, to think and to gift us the benefit of their considered philosophies on life, love, friendship, selflessness and the myriad other virtues we humans are capable of.*

AND VANESSA FELTZ

My Pause for Thought *is broadcast when many people are just getting out of bed, so it's an inspiring start to the day.*

Every week we delve into a different theme, which contributors interpret in their highly individual ways. The variety is outstanding.

It's fascinating to find out what makes our lovely listeners 'pause for thought' and we love it when they send in photos of the 'wow' moments, when they really were stopped in their tracks. You'll find some of those brilliant images in this book, and there are many more in the Listener Gallery on the Pause for Thought *homepage.*

Pause For Thought *often surprises, intrigues, generates discussion, delights and, we hope, inspires. This compilation contains a giant slug of wisdom we believe will encourage you to stop, relax and consider the more fundamental things in life.*

1

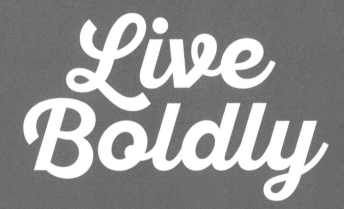

'THE ASTRONAUTS
LOWER THEIR VOICES
AND MARVEL AT A
VIEW THAT CHANGES
THE WAY YOU SEE
EVERYTHING.'

Richard Coles

RICHARD COLES

BROADCASTER AND VICAR OF FINEDON IN NORTHAMPTONSHIRE

Broadcast 09:20 | 12 December 2014

Three carol services this week, and we sang three times of the star of Bethlehem, westward leading through the night skies of Palestine to the birth of Christ. I thought of the night skies of Finedon, my parish, and me and my eight-year-old neighbour Hattie standing in the garden, looking at the International Space Station, westward leading on its orbit of Earth.

'Wave to the astronauts,' I said, and she waved and so did I.

I've renewed that acquaintance this week, but in proximity rather than at a distance. In fact, the Space Station's former Commander, Chris Hadfield, and I have spent so much time together lately people are beginning to talk.

We met on Monday, to discuss science and religion, among other things, so speaking sky-pilot to sky-pilot I asked, 'What's Christmas like in space?'

'Complicated,' was the answer.

The Space Station orbits the Earth at 17,000 miles per hour — rather a challenge for Rudolf and his reindeer pals to catch up with that — but there are presents, double helpings actually, because the Russians on board, following the Julian calendar, keep Christmas on a different day. Thanks to the mission safety protocols, crackers are definitely out, but there is a Christmas tree, looking a bit tatty now, he said, and disappointingly no bigger than a poinsettia.

However, the best thing, he said, was going to the Cupola, the 360-degree observation dome, and looking out at Planet Earth in the vast blackness of space, so fragile, so beautiful that the astronauts lower their voices and speak in hushed tones, marvelling at a view that changes the way you see everything.

And I thought then of the Wise Men, led by
a star to a crib, and looking into its radiance,

and seeing a tiny baby,
so fragile, so beautiful;
and how that changed
the way they saw
everything.

O Magnum Mysterium, *O Great Mystery that comes*
out of nowhere and lights the stars and sends
them spinning into space!

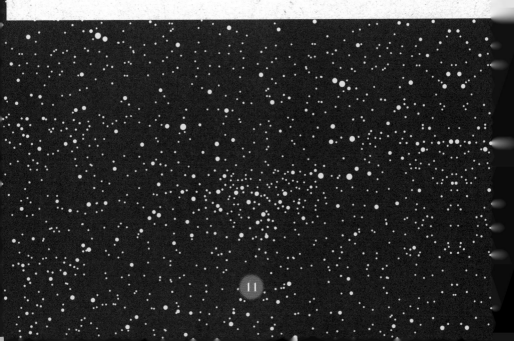

'LIFE'S JOURNEY IS THERE IN ALL GOOD STORIES.'

Paul Kerensa

PAUL KERENSA
COMEDIAN AND WRITER

Broadcast 09.20 | 25 February 2015

As a writer, I love stories and finding out how they work, and handily some writers write about writing, Christopher Vogler and Joseph Campbell being two favourites. They suggest that many great stories follow a pattern. An ordinary world spawns a call to adventure: Hagrid turns up at Harry Potter's house; Luke Skywalker hears Princess Leia's cry for help. The hero's unsure but meets a Dumbledorian, Gandalfy, Obi-Wanish mentor, tries initial tasks, makes allies, trusts and distrusts, plays their own personal Hunger Games. They face their greatest foe in a supreme ordeal — a light-sabre-off with Darth Vader — or glimpse the wizard behind the curtain. Finally, it's the road home, to Kansas, Hobbiton or back through the wardrobe. Our hero is changed, rewarded, with a reminder it wasn't a dream. This story pattern reflects life and all its challenges. The world of our youth may feel comfortable or we may grow up quickly.

When we tiptoe into life's adventure, there are risks, mentors and foes. We face insurmountable challenges but survive and come back stronger.

Life's journey is there in all good stories, I think even in the Bible — The Greatest Story Ever Told (although Inception was quite good too). You could argue The Good Book also echoes life's story pattern: a comfortable, perfect world gives way to tests, allies, enemies; and when the challenge becomes too great for us, Jesus journeys to the darkest point, the innermost cave — death — from where he rises. As in that story pattern, something is left behind: the message and spirit, a reminder that it's not a dream.

Perhaps I'm over-theorising — we humans put patterns on everything. But I think our life stories find echoes in all culture — even in your fine show, Chris. Bear with me! Your show's birth follows Vanessa, the mother-figure. Like children, we try things for the first time. Some days bring us sunshine; others, mystery guests. There are gobsmacking moments, times of sport and unexpected breaking news ... And by the end of it, hopefully we find time to pause for thought.

OMAR HAMDI
COMEDIAN

Broadcast 00:45 | 29 June 2014

*We all want to get ahead. Whether you're a
panicky intern on your first Monday morning
coffee run, a workaholic captain of industry
planning your next acquisition or, like me, a
comedian wanting to play bigger venues, we all
look to the next step up.*

*A lot has been said about how it's tougher to get
ahead today if you don't have the right parents,
didn't go to the right school or don't have the
right accent. Sometimes it seems like faith has
no place in this world — faith is something for
monks in their monasteries, the most extra-
curricular of activities.*

*The world of showbusiness seemed a million miles
away when I was growing up on the outskirts of
Cardiff with a single mum and neighbours I didn't
have much in common with. I was a slightly geeky,
slightly hyper Egyptian boy. But I always felt*

that I belonged on stage or in the studio as much as anyone else. It can't be a coincidence that, in the Abrahamic religions, prophets have almost always been underdogs or outsiders. Read their life stories, and, whether you are illiterate like Muhammad, born into poverty like Jesus or wandering through your own personal desert like Moses, you can see a path of aspiration and hope.

Even if you are not personally religious, these people were and are figureheads of global religions, and they never had a leg up.

The only 'old boy' they knew was the oldest boy of them all: God.

Ambition and wanting to fulfil our potential wasn't invented by city traders. 'Self-help' isn't a creation of 20th-century authors.

When I get on stage for a stand-up gig, I know I can do it, because so could Muhammad, Jesus and Moses. The way I see it, I don't need the right parents, the right school or the right accent, but I do need faith in God and in myself.

'WHEN I GET ON STAGE FOR A STAND-UP GIG, I KNOW I CAN DO IT, BECAUSE SO COULD MUHAMMAD, JESUS AND MOSES.'

Omar Hamdi

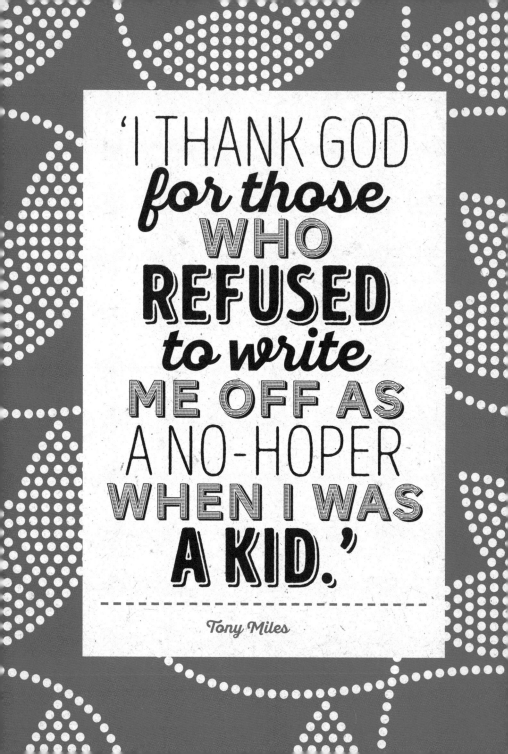

TONY MILES

MINISTER AND MEDIA CHAPLAIN OF
METHODIST CENTRAL HALL, WESTMINSTER

Broadcast 05.45 | 11 September 2015

*When I preach at my church, I often think
'What on earth am I doing here? If only people
knew that I failed my RE exams at school!'
It's humbling and challenging to think of the
impressive line-up of movers and shakers who've
spoken in our Great Hall over the years. There's
the great wartime preacher Dr William Sangster,
for example. There's Martin Luther King, the
Dalai Lama and Sir Winston Churchill. Other
visitors to Methodist Central Hall, Westminster,
include those who formed the inaugural meeting
of the United Nations in 1946, our now longest-
reigning monarch, and Mahatma Gandhi, too!*

*Gandhi, the Father of his Nation, was the
spiritual and political leader who coordinated
and led India's successful national struggle
for independence against British imperial rule
— all by way of a non-violent movement. 'If you*

want real peace in the world,' he said, 'start with children.'

Looking back, I thank God for those who refused to write me off as a no-hoper when I was a kid. People who believed that 'all matter', who worked with the raw material and patiently invested in my future.

So, just as people helped us, my wife and I have tried to do likewise for others. One way has been to set aside a relatively small amount to help children, including in India.

We were inspired by true stories of transformed lives.

Take Jane (pronounced 'ja-nay'), for example. He was born in Kolkata's Mollahati slum, where 10,000 people shared two toilets and just one tap. Yet, with the help of sponsorship, Jane became the first child in his entire community to go to school. Later, it took him just a single year to get a Masters in International Business with first class honours! Now he's making a difference to other people's lives himself.

'You may never know what results come of your action,' Gandhi once said,

'but if you do nothing there will be no result.'

This is something that rattles my complacency as I watch the heart-rending images on the news of children among the refugees and migrants. All matter!

Okay, I will never be numbered among the great and good, but I believe I can, with God's help, make a difference to others, through compassion and generosity. In Gandhi's words, 'A small body of determined spirits fired by an unquenchable faith in their mission can alter the course of history.'

'Beneath our deepest
fears is a well of hope
and courage that we
can all access while
listening quietly to our
higher instincts.'

Jeff Berger

JEFF BERGER

RABBI OF THE RAMBAM SEPHARDI
SYNAGOGUE, BOREHAMWOOD

Broadcast 00:45 | 28 June 2015

On one occasion, when I was nine years old, the telephone rang during dinner. News arrived that our uncle had been rushed to hospital after suffering a major heart attack at the theatre. The call set off a frenzy of activity and caused my parents great distress. This was the first time the threat of death intruded into my childhood, and the fear of it sent me upstairs to my room to pray quietly that he would survive.

I am rabbi of a small community in Hertfordshire, and one afternoon in 2011 the phone rang. The male caller sounded anguished. He apologised but needed to speak with a rabbi urgently — his mother-in-law was dying. That long-forgotten childhood fear instantly pierced my heart. And although we trained for this inevitability in the seminary, I felt unprepared. Curbing a sense of panic, I asked for details, promising to ring

him back shortly. Immediately, I called a mentor
who rehearsed the rituals with me and then added,
'Stay calm and trust your better instincts.'

When I arrived, the son-in-law explained that
the lady, nearly 90 years old, had decided to
stop eating a few days earlier and was slowly
but peacefully slipping into unconsciousness.
The end-of-life ritual in Judaism is probably
similar to those in other religions — a brief
confessional prayer and a few minutes of
chanting. But I sensed more was needed. Though
we'd never met, I took this sweet lady's hand
instinctively and began singing sacred melodies
that she would know well. After about 20
minutes, when all seemed tearful but calm, I left
discretely. Sadly, a few days later, the family
asked if I would conduct the funeral.

Since then there have been more than a hundred
calls, each requiring its own response. We face
many fears in life — the fear of death perhaps
the hardest. But that first occasion helped me to
realise that beneath our deepest fears is a well
of hope and courage that we can all access while
listening quietly to our higher instincts.

BRIAN D'ARCY

CATHOLIC PASSIONIST PRIEST AND WRITER

Broadcast 09:20 | 7 October 2013

When I trained for the priesthood 50 years ago, I was warned that the world around me would change but my values should remain the same. For years I lived by that principle until I realised I would become mentally and emotionally ill unless I abandoned such dark-age philosophy.

Everything changes, and that includes me.

Now, no matter how I try to avoid it, I have to admit that 'change' and 'choice' are part of life; both are to be welcomed, not feared. However, so much changes so rapidly these days that I can't possibly keep abreast of it all. I'm one of the dwindling few who still remember when phones had wires attached and when notebooks required pens. I'm also the first to admit that almost all the changes that I once resisted have made life easier and better.

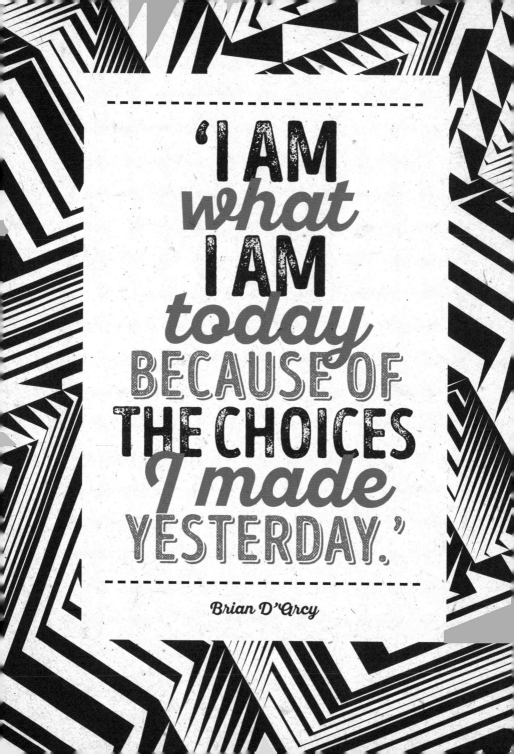

Yet even today, when I'm faced with a new project which forces me to leave my comfort zone, my gut feeling is to give up. I have to remind myself that both change and choice keep me young at heart and that without them I'd become a dead fish in a stagnant pond.

The French philosopher Jean-Paul Sartre agreed when he stated, 'We are our choices.' I am what I am today because of the choices I made yesterday, and, at this stage in my life, it's vital that I welcome change and that I actually make choices rather than being paralysed by so many options. To do nothing is in itself a choice — the decision not to choose — and usually the worst one.

For me, a wrong choice is braver than no choice at all.

It's easier to make good decisions, though, when you know what your principles are. So embrace change, make choices, know your core principles and, above all, choose what is right and honest.

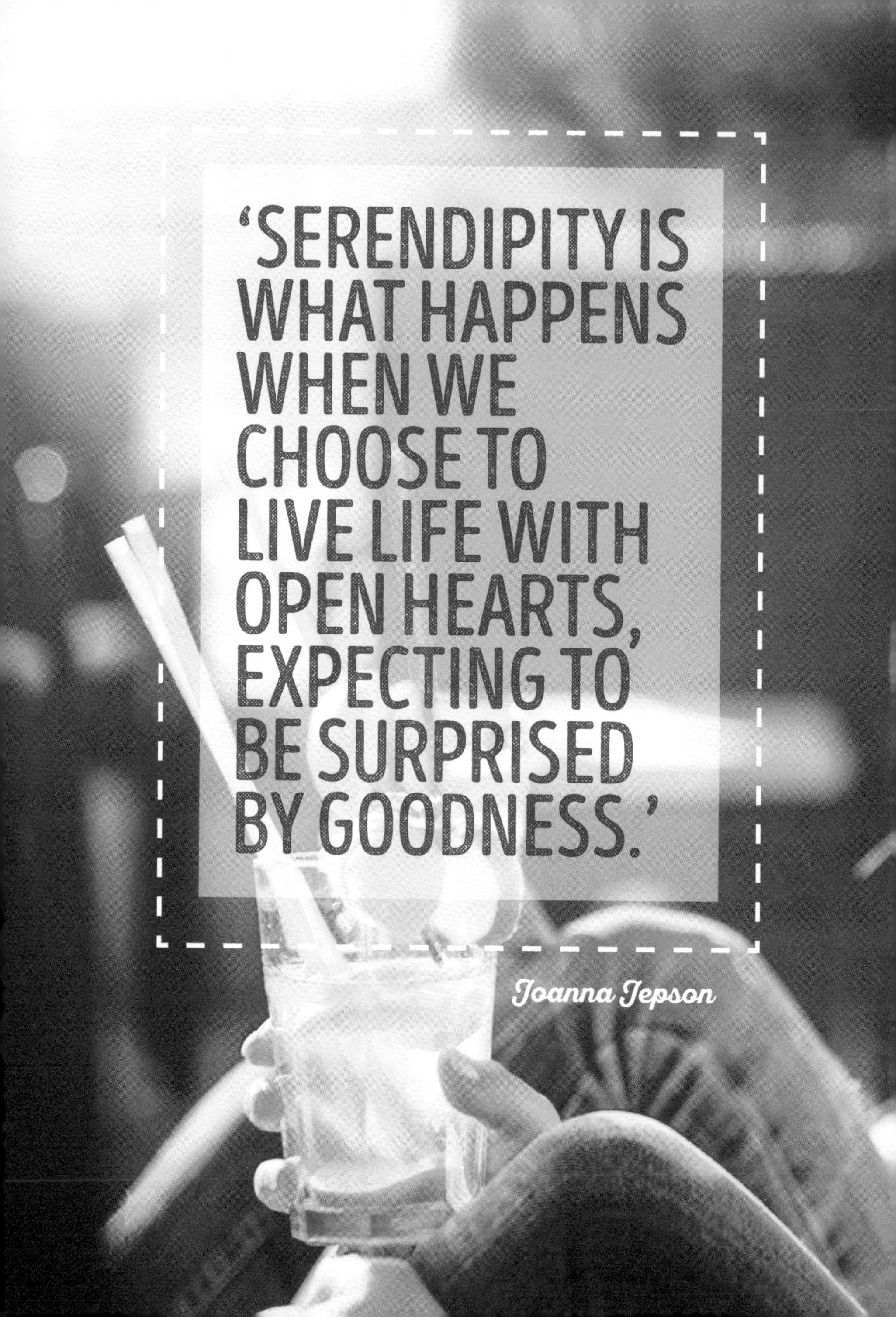
'SERENDIPITY IS WHAT HAPPENS WHEN WE CHOOSE TO LIVE LIFE WITH OPEN HEARTS, EXPECTING TO BE SURPRISED BY GOODNESS.'
Joanna Jepson

JOANNA JEPSON

ANGLICAN PRIEST AND AUTHOR

Broadcast 00:45 | 12 April 2016

*It was a warm evening as my friends and I headed
to the local bar on the island of Santorini. When
we arrived it was too early for the hard-core
clubbers, and as we got the drinks in and enjoyed
the music there was space for us to chat before
being caught up in the crowds and heavy beats.*

*My friend noticed her first. The girl was
standing not far from us, nursing a drink as she
smiled at us a little uncertainly. She didn't
strike me as an all-out party animal. 'Go over
and talk to her,' my friend urged, 'she's by
herself.' So I did; I asked her if she wanted to
come and join us. We gathered her into our little
group and later she told me that she had suffered
a long illness and going travelling by herself
was her way of celebrating her new-found health.
'It's my way of saying to the universe I am going
to live life to the full and not be afraid.'*

I listened to her story and thought how courageous she was, even just for taking the step to go to a bar by herself when it seemed everyone else had friends to be with. Then she said, 'I knew it would be okay. I felt this sense that God would meet me and look after me. And he did.'

I've often thought about that girl and her courage and her willingness to say 'yes' to life while trusting that God would show up. There's a verse in the Book of Romans that says all things work together for the good for those who love God. Which is another way of saying, 'Don't lose heart, make space for hope!

Nothing is too broken or hopeless for God to transform!'

I think that serendipity is what happens when we choose to live life with open hearts, expecting to be surprised by goodness.

Live Boldly!

Verbier,
Switzerland

Janice Nice

Auchterarder,
Perthshire

Joanna Wallace

Bath, Somerset

Rebecca Lawrence

Straws Bridge,
Derbyshire

Thomas Leleux

Bridport, Dorset

Andrew Oliver

Mam Tor,
Derbyshire

Robin Greenwell

Photographs taken by **Pause for Thought** listeners of
some of the things that made them stop and think (visit
the **Pause for Thought** homepage for more great images)

Understand

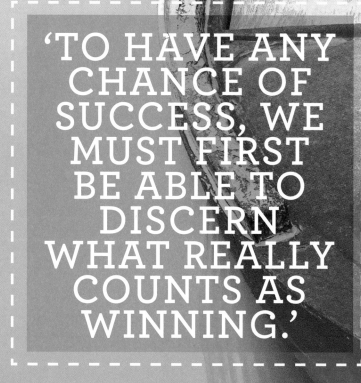

'TO HAVE ANY CHANCE OF SUCCESS, WE MUST FIRST BE ABLE TO DISCERN WHAT REALLY COUNTS AS WINNING.'

Shelina Janmohamed

SHELINA JANMOHAMED
AUTHOR AND BLOGGER

Broadcast 00:45 | 12 July 2014

A banker was standing on the pier of an Italian fishing village, when a small fishing boat docked. 'How long did it take you to catch those?' the banker asked the fisherman, referring to several large, beautiful fish in the boat. 'Just a short while,' the fisherman replied. The banker was surprised he hadn't stayed out longer to catch more fish, but the fisherman explained that this amount was enough to support his family. 'What do you do with the rest of your time?' asked the baffled banker.

'I sleep late, fish a little, play with my children, take siestas with my wife and stroll into the village each evening where I play guitar with my friends.'

The banker scoffed, 'I have an MBA and could help you. If you fish more, you could buy a bigger boat, then several boats and eventually a fleet.

Then you could buy a factory, control processing and distribution and even expand globally.' 'How long will this take?' asked the fisherman. 'Maybe 15 or 20 years,' replied the banker. 'Then what?' 'You could sell your company and make millions.' 'Then what?'

'Then,' smiled the banker, 'you could retire and move to a small Italian fishing village where you could sleep late, fish a little, play with your children, take siestas with your wife and stroll into the village each evening and play guitar with your friends.'

It's so easy to see winning in monetary terms or to set our goals by the markers of success that our culture defines for us — houses, jobs with status, glamorous holidays and nice clothes. But the winners are those who see what the endgame is rather than playing by the rules of others. We can be blinded to the real goal by what seem to be 'wins' along the way. The Qur'an sums this up in a simple, memorable way: 'Is the blind equal to the one who sees? Or darkness equal to light?' To have any chance of success, we must first be able to discern what really counts as winning.

DEBBIE YOUNG-SOMERS

RABBI AND COMMUNITY EDUCATOR AT THE
MOVEMENT FOR REFORM JUDAISM

Broadcast 00:45 | 13 March 2015

I remember very clearly one of the first times
my mum taught me something that would remain
with me for life.

I was seven years old and my mum was a supply
teacher assigned to my form. As my sister had
an inset day from her school, she came with her.
That afternoon one of my classmates asked me what
was wrong with my sister.

I didn't know what to say. I didn't know there
was anything wrong with her.

She was just my sister.

After some tears, when we were safely home, I
asked my mum the same question: what WAS wrong
with my sister? Rather than her trying to explain
it to me, she asked my sister to tell me.

And Sara took up the challenge and explained that
when she was born, the water travelling around
her head had become stuck, causing some brain
damage and making her head misshapen — something
my classmate had obviously spotted rather quicker
than me.

My mum gave my sister the dignity of speaking
herself, rather than talking about it without her
as if it were a bad thing or a secret.

Sara could own her challenges

and I knew I could speak directly to her
about them.

This episode has repeatedly reminded me to allow
people the dignity of speaking for themselves
rather than speaking about them or around them.
Even when we might assume people don't have
the ability to speak for themselves or might be
uncomfortable doing so, we actually give them a
huge gift when we invite them to own their story
and tell it themselves.

'WE GIVE people a huge GIFT WHEN we invite THEM TO own their STORY AND TELL IT themselves.'

Debbie Young-Somers

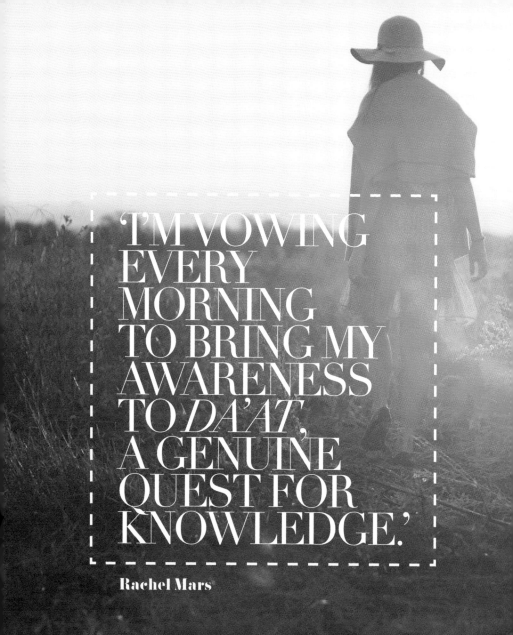

'I'M VOWING EVERY MORNING TO BRING MY AWARENESS TO *DA'AT*, A GENUINE QUEST FOR KNOWLEDGE.'

Rachel Mars

RACHEL MARS

PERFORMER AND WRITER

Broadcast 00:45 | 21 October 2014

*In Judaism there are daily morning prayers.
One of them is the prayer for* da'at, *meaning
'knowledge'. It's a sort of petition for greater
insight and a thank you for the ability to go
on in pursuit of knowledge.*

*I've never been religious enough to have a
morning ritual of prayer, but recently I've found
that I've developed a troubling new morning
ritual of my own. Reaching for my phone to see
what time it is, I flick onto my social-media
newsfeed to see what is happening in the world.
I start the day with photos, links, videos and
opinions — so many opinions — and this summer,
with all the geopolitical crises and debates
regarding Syria, ISIS and Israel, my newsfeed
changed shape.*

*At its best, my newsfeed alerted me to a well-
considered, challenging article or an analyst*

*I'd not heard of. At its worst it read like
an inflammatory radio phone-in — outraged and
ill-informed views clamouring for space among
selfies, boasts disguised as self-deprecation
and videos of cats on vacuum cleaners.*

*Yes, I remind myself, everyone is entitled to
their opinions, but when it comes to knowledge
not all opinions have the same weight. With the
speed at which we can now access information, the
need to question our sources has been replaced
with the need to answer our questions. We're at
risk of no longer checking our facts, reading
around the issue and challenging our perceptions.
It's so much easier to skim-read something and
hit 'share'.*

*So, while I might not reach for a prayer book,
I'm vowing every morning to bring my awareness
to da'at, a genuine quest for knowledge, and not
one centred on social media. It will be a daily
commitment to seeking out various sources, to
fact-check and question what I'm being presented
with and to not be seduced by the speed, ease and
ultimate ignorance of the re-post.*

KIERA PHYO

YOUTH DIRECTOR AT TEARFUND, AN
INTERNATIONAL DEVELOPMENT CHARITY

Broadcast 05.45 | 17 February 2014

Like most small children who are taken furniture
shopping with their parents, my four-year-old
self grumbled with boredom as I walked sluggishly
behind my mum. It was a welcome distraction to
see another child also skulking in her mother's
shadow. I waved tentatively and was delighted
when we started walking towards each other,
hopeful for some like-minded company. I was all
but a couple of feet from her when I realised
that she was, in fact, me. I had no new friend,
just an unrecognised reflection of myself.

Even now — although I am fooled by mirrors less
often — there are many times when I look at
myself and have an inaccurate view of the person
looking back at me. I read in the paper recently
that 70 per cent of people will suffer from the
'imposter syndrome' at some point in their lives.
It refers to the sensation that we're faking

'**I'M NOT** an imposter, **A FAKE OR** a fraud: **I'M JUST SOMEONE** giving it **A GO LIKE EVERYONE** ELSE.'

Kiera Phyo

it; that, despite our successes, achievements or whatever we've done in life, we still think we're not good enough and any day now we're going to get caught. We feel like frauds.

At this year's Grammy Awards, when the fabulously talented singer—songwriter Sara Bareilles was nominated for 'Album of the Year', she said, 'I've always had impostor syndrome, like I don't really belong here ... I keep waiting for someone to tap me on the shoulder and be like "Uh, you have to go."' Her words make me think how often we don't see ourselves for who we really are. I may always struggle to ignore the insecurities I see in myself, but when my reflection looks like a frazzled mum or an under-confident worker, my faith tells me that I don't have to be perfect to be worth something, and that my errors (and they are daily!) don't lessen my value. I'm not an imposter, a fake or a fraud; I'm just giving it a go like everyone else. I believe God sees not my reflection but my true self, made in his likeness. And I know his message is that I am loved and worthy, but on the days when that is hard to believe, I'll muster the courage and be happy enough to settle with thinking I'm okay.

'Sometimes, mystery is good. Mystery is not darkness.'

Jim Harris

JIM HARRIS
ART HISTORIAN AND TEACHING CURATOR AT THE ASHMOLEAN MUSEUM

Broadcast 09:20 | 17 November 2015

One of the best things about my job is meeting experts. The Ashmolean Museum, where I work, is full of them, and so is the rest of Oxford. The people I teach alongside are specialists in history, modern languages, theology, classics, neuroscience, geography, literature and all sorts of other things, and they seem to know everything. It's the greatest treat imaginable to work with them.

Some days, though — and yesterday was one — it's the hardest stretch to keep up with them. I feel as if, no matter how much I learn, it'll never be enough and I'll always be slightly in the dark. In fact, this seems like an appropriate metaphor for my whole life at the moment, since, at this time of the year, I get up in the dark, travel to work in the dark and leave work in the dark.

The thing is, while I'm certain that learning is good, I'm also pretty sure that we simply can't know everything. In the Book of Proverbs, the author says that there are four things he doesn't understand: the way of an eagle in the sky, the way of a snake on a rock, the way of a ship on the sea and the way of a man with a young woman.

Now, those are indeed mysterious things, as anyone who's ever watched a David Attenborough documentary, been on a boat out of sight of land or been in love will know. But, sometimes, mystery is good. Mystery is not darkness. There is beauty, intrigue and wonder in it, as well as the truth of what it is to be human.

So when we don't understand what we see, I reckon this can do two great things. Firstly, it can make us amazed at this wonderful world, which, even when it's dark, is an astonishing place to live. Secondly, it can set off the spark of curiosity that makes us want to learn more about it. And the more we understand the world and each other,

the more amazing these become.

KRISHNA DHARMA
HINDU PRIEST AND AUTHOR

Broadcast 00:45 | 7 May 2015

Over the years my idea of victory has changed
somewhat. In my younger days, filled with the
naïve certainty of youth, I saw myself conquering
the world, acquiring vast riches, fame and all
that sort of thing. That ambition has been rather
tempered by reality, as it tends to be,

but I no longer see
world conquest as even
a desirable victory.

Of course, my view of success depends on what
I value most, and, as a young man, material
achievements were high up on my list. This tends
to be the paradigm instilled in us by modern
living: earn more, have more and find more
happiness. Over the years, though, I've come to
understand that having more things in this world
— whether they are possessions, fame or fortune

— will never make me happy. That seems to be the case for many of us, and indeed our consumer society is built upon this fundamental fact. If we were satisfied with the phone, car, clothes or whatever it is we own, then many industries would dry up pretty quickly. Thankfully for them, though, we are not so easily contented. In the universal search for that bit more happiness, society appears to crave the latest and best model of everything, and business is booming.

Lao Tzu, the great Chinese philosopher, said: 'He has the most who wants the least.' In other words, what we really want is contentment and peace of mind. We're hoping that our acquisitions will somehow make us happy, but that never seems to happen. For this reason, the ancient Hindu treatise Bhagavad Gita says that only one who subdues the ever-demanding senses can be at peace, not one who strives to satisfy them. One whose mind is not controlled won't be happy owning even the entire Earth. For this reason I now see victory as conquering my own material desires, turning away from the things of this world, towards the spirit within. That, to me, would be the greatest possible victory.

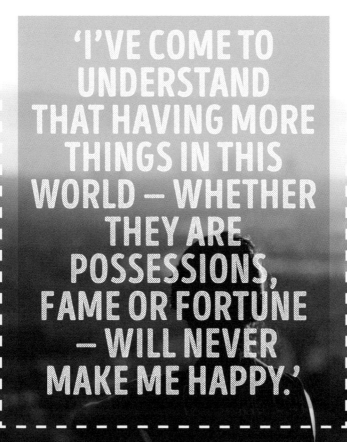

'I'VE COME TO
UNDERSTAND
THAT HAVING MORE
THINGS IN THIS
WORLD – WHETHER
THEY ARE
POSSESSIONS,
FAME OR FORTUNE
– WILL NEVER
MAKE ME HAPPY.'

Krishna Dharma

PAM RHODES
SONGS OF PRAISE PRESENTER

Broadcast 05:45 | 17 April 2015

Seventy years on from the end of World War II, this week we recall how liberation finally came to the prisoners in those inhuman concentration camps. I remember some years ago going round The Holocaust Exhibition at the Imperial War Museum with Jonathan Sachs, who was then the Chief Rabbi. I asked him, 'Six million killed; people of faith. Where was God?' And his answer has stayed with me:

'The question is not where was God, but where was man?'

When I think of his response now, it takes me back to an event that took place when I was a youngster. I lived on an estate where all the houses circled around an area of grass that was a playground for kids, watched by parents in

every household. One day there was great upset
when a bossy boy pinched a smaller lad's bike
and ended up buckling the wheel. The bike's owner
immediately burst into tears — but then we all
knew him to be a cry baby, so we just watched
from the sidelines as the big boy taunted him.

Suddenly, into the crowd marched Nan, our
formidable grandmother. One by one, she asked
us all what we thought of the big boy, and
eventually the word 'bully' was mentioned by
just about everyone. When she spoke of the
smaller boy, we told her he was always a cry
baby, so she asked us why he cried so often and
if we knew anything about him that might make him
unhappy. And we did know — that his dad had died
so his mum was bringing up four children on her
own; that they all shared hand-me-downs which we
often made fun of; and that the only bike we'd
ever seen any of them use was the one which was
now in front of us, broken.

We felt so ashamed. Then Nan said, 'Every single
one of us is shaped by our circumstances, and
unless you can imagine yourself in his shoes and
understand what he's been through and how he's

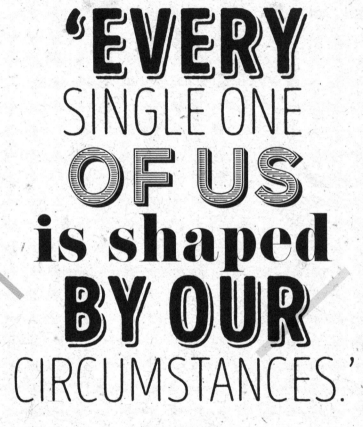

'**EVERY** SINGLE ONE **OF US** is shaped **BY OUR** CIRCUMSTANCES.'

Pam Rhodes

feeling, you've no right to judge or bully.
And you lot standing around are just as bad!
You knew something wrong was happening and
you did nothing. That makes you no better than
that bully!'

I often think of her words these days when there's so much bullying going on around the world.

Because I think the problems are too huge for my
opinion to matter, I see myself standing back
watching what I know to be wrong – and doing
nothing. I can't blame God for that; that's down
to me. I'm glad Nan can't see me now ...

3

CHALLENGE
PRECONCEPTIONS

'A TRUE KINGSHIP
IS TO RULE WITH THE
HEART AND HEAD
OF BOTH A KING
AND A QUEEN.'

Onjali Rauf

ONJALI RAUF

FOUNDER AND CEO OF THE WOMEN'S RIGHTS CHARITY MAKING HERSTORY

Broadcast 00:45 | 19 October 2015

Even as a child, whenever faced with a word with 'king' in it — 'kingdom', 'kingsmen', 'kingship' — an innate part of me has always risen up with a sword in hand to ask, 'What about queendoms? Or queenships? And why aren't we called 'the United Queendom' when we have a queen on the throne? What's that all about?'

As childish as those questions may seem, they stemmed from a deep uneasiness at the feeling that women had a lesser role to play in leadership. After all, all our prophets, from Abraham to Moses to Muhammad, were 'kings among men'. And if God was 'King' of all the worlds and a 'He' in every sense of the word, did that not mean all 'hes' were better than 'shes', and therefore kingships better than queen-anythings? As I grew older, the weight of such questions grew heavier, and before long I found myself looking hungrily to God and the Qur'an for answers about leadership in relation to men and women. To my great surprise, I came to find that 'kingship' in the world of God was not as I had been brought up to understand it.

I FOUND THAT MY GOD WAS IN FACT A GENDERLESS RULER,

not the bearded, crowned man sat on a throne as I had imagined, but a Being whose rules and actions encompassed qualities traditionally associated with both men and women.

So now the terms 'king' and 'kingship' have taken on a new meaning. For any of us to govern justly, we need to have the skills to both lead and serve; to be strong yet compassionate and merciful. We also have to be noble and possess humility. In other words, a true kingship is to rule with the heart and head of both a king and a queen. And that's a form of kingship I can definitely live with!

KRISH RAVAL
YOUTH LEADERSHIP COACH

Broadcast 00:45 | 4 November 2014

My grandmother died a few weeks ago at the age
of 97 in her native India. A devout woman of
indomitable spirit, she once remarked that, for
her, the source of both happiness and suffering
was the same.

When she was 81 years old, she and her youngest
son (my uncle) went to worship at a local Hindu
shrine. During their return, as my uncle steered
his vehicle along the desolate and jagged track
home, their car overturned. My grandmother was
flung entirely through the windscreen and my
uncle hit his head on a milestone.

Although bloody and bruised, incredibly, the
injuries my grandmother sustained were minor. As
she tended to her unconscious son, she prayed for
help. And it came. Working in the fields were
farmhands who rushed to the scene. They carefully
pushed the two casualties on a milk cart until
they found a car to take them to hospital.

*Heartbreakingly, we lost my uncle on that
journey. Yet my family and I will never forget
that the heroes who had aided him and my
grandmother were Muslims, Hindus and Jains who
had instinctively mounted a multi-faith relief
operation. It was as if tragedy had focused my
family and their rescuers on the best of what it
means to be human — to give and receive help.*

THEIR MUTUAL EMPATHY WENT DEEPER THAN ANY DIVISIONS.

*For Hindus, happiness at its most basic level
will inevitably be temporary and lead to
suffering. Prompted perhaps by unspeakable loss
and the goodness of perfect strangers, towards
the end of her life my grandmother saw true
happiness not in the elimination of all harm, but
rather in the wholeness that comes from seeing
oneself as connected to others. Such happiness
endures precisely because it is not focused on
the demands of the self but is in service to the
rest of creation.*

'My grandmother saw true happiness not in the elimination of all harm, but rather in the wholeness that comes from seeing oneself as connected to others.'

Krish Raval

ROBERT HARRAP
GENERAL DIRECTOR OF SGI-UK, A SOCIALLY ENGAGED BUDDHIST MOVEMENT

Broadcast 05.45 | 8 January 2015

There's a short poem by John Keats that I really love. It's called 'On First Looking into Chapman's Homer', and in it the poet describes his feelings of excitement upon reading a new translation of an old, classic text. He compares this feeling to the surprise an astronomer might have on discovering a new planet, or to the reaction of an explorer when he finally sees the thing he has been searching for after battling over unknown mountains and through strange jungles. Keats suggests that even things we know quite well can suddenly reveal new wonder when we look at them in a different way, perhaps through someone else's eyes.

When I was growing up, I thought that a successful and happy life would be one that didn't have any problems or difficulties. Perhaps, I thought, I could create a barrier around me through which problems wouldn't be able to penetrate. I quickly realised, though, that this wasn't possible and that it was actually a pretty deluded approach to life, which is always going to have its ups and downs.

When I started to explore Buddhist writings, I came across a phrase that stuck with me, and which has become a sort of motto for my life:

TRUE HAPPINESS IS NOT THE ABSENCE OF ALL PROBLEMS, BUT RATHER THE ABSOLUTE CONFIDENCE THAT ANY PROBLEM CAN BE RESOLVED.

The first time I read it, I thought it must have been a typing error — surely I can't be happy if I have problems? However, I started to experiment to see if this could be true.

As problems emerged I decided to see them as opportunities to draw out my inner potential. I saw that every problem is in fact a challenge,

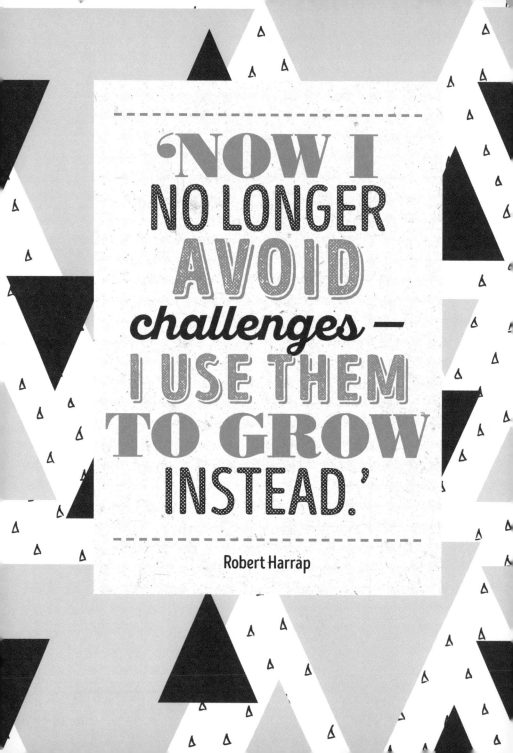

'NOW I NO LONGER AVOID challenges — I USE THEM TO GROW INSTEAD.'

Robert Harrap

with the opportunity for me to grow and to develop a bigger view, a bigger heart and a bigger perspective.

I remember a time a few years ago when, at the place where I was then working, someone more senior than me was throwing their weight around unnecessarily. When I realised that it wasn't actually my fault and that this person must be suffering to behave in that way, I was able to draw on my compassion rather than on my anger, and interact with them in a very different way – and the situation resolved.

THIS CHANGE IN ATTITUDE WAS A WONDERFUL DISCOVERY.

Now I no longer avoid challenges – I use them to grow instead.

'Rap music and Sikhism essentially have a similar goal — to give a voice to the voiceless and to encourage change in the way we live for the better.'

Harwinder Singh

HARWINDER SINGH
PROJECT COORDINATOR IN THE
SIKH COMMUNITY

Broadcast 00:45 | 7 January 2014

The first album I ever purchased was a
compilation cassette tape titled Rap Attack.
I was 12 years old and, after seeing adverts for
it on television, I knew I had to go out and buy
it. For months beforehand, I'd been listening to
bootlegged rap music that had been copied onto
second-hand cassette tapes, and I was starting to
take a keen interest in this revolutionary style
from rappers with names like Snoop Doggy Dogg
and Ice Cube. But unlike the album I bought, what
I had been listening to so far was uncensored,
explicit and certainly inappropriate for someone
of my age. As a result, I was careful to ensure
those tapes weren't left lying around in case
my parents accidentally played them and got the
shock of their lives!

As I was growing up and being introduced to the
Sikh way of life, I noticed that there were

a number of similarities between the vocal expression that exudes from rap music and the reformist zeal of Guru Nanak, founder of Sikhism.

He, like the rappers of the past few decades, wrote poetry about the life around him

AND THE PROMISE OF A BETTER WORLD IF WE CAN MAKE CHANGES TO THE *STATUS QUO.*

Sikhism flourished under the Guru's guidance, and the challenge to put his teachings into practice is one that I face every day.

Rap music still has a bad reputation and is all too often associated with violence, misogyny and greed. I believe this is an undeserved stereotype based on just a portion of the music published. Because of that stereotype, listening to rap music while trying to be a good Sikh might appear to be a difficult task from the outside, but they essentially have a similar goal: to give a voice to the voiceless and to encourage change in the way we live for the better.

MIKE STARKEY
WRITER AND BROADCASTER

Broadcast 00:45 | 18 February 2015

There's no question that we're richer and healthier now than people were 50 years ago. We have hi-definition TVs and cinemas with a dozen screens. We have access to more music than any society ever, better transport and a variety of clothing that for most of history would have been the preserve of royalty.

NEVER BEFORE HAVE WE PURSUED THE GOAL OF HAPPINESS SO RELENTLESSLY.

The strange thing is, though, surveys show we're no happier than we were 50 years ago. We have higher levels of depression than any other society in history. We can buy something that gives us pleasure — a chocolate bar, perhaps, or a new car — and it lifts our mood briefly but it doesn't last. Psychologists say we 'adapt to *pleasure'; our level of happiness or contentment doesn't stay raised and it soon drops back to its earlier stage.*

Not surprisingly, people who live in extreme poverty do experience lower levels of happiness. But, interestingly, research shows that once you get the basics of a life — home, food and clothes — having more money and more stuff makes no further difference to your level of happiness. And the cut-off point seems to be an income of just £10,000 a year.

ABOVE THAT POINT, NO INCREASE SEEMS TO MAKE ANY DIFFERENCE TO HOW HAPPY YOU FEEL.

This week marks the start of Lent: that season of waiting in the run-up to Easter. Traditionally, people give up something, such as alcohol or chocolate. I prefer to think of it as a great time to simplify my life; to do a bit of decluttering. That, in turn, helps me concentrate on what real happiness is all about.

'ONCE YOU GET THE BASICS of a life HAVING MORE MONEY AND MORE STUFF MAKES NO DIFFERENCE to your HAPPINESS.'

Mike Starkey

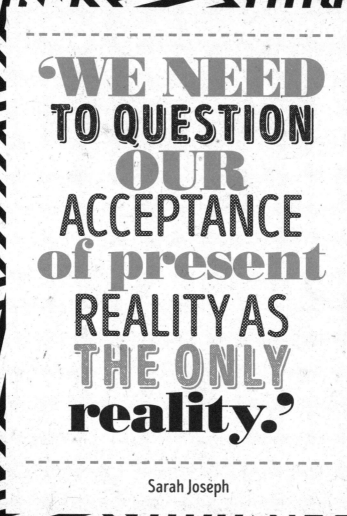

'WE NEED TO QUESTION OUR ACCEPTANCE of present REALITY AS THE ONLY reality.'

Sarah Joseph

SARAH JOSEPH
WRITER AND EDITOR

Broadcast 09:20 | 9 October 2014

*It was Eid on Saturday and the culmination of
the Hajj, one of the largest gatherings of
pilgrims on Earth. The pilgrims fulfil rituals in
remembrance of the prophet Abraham, who is a key
figure in Judaism, Christianity and Islam. There
are many stories about him in Muslim tradition
— indeed, a whole chapter of the Qur'an is named
after him. It describes his sacrifices, his
doubts and questionings, his remarkable faith in
God and the way he stood up to the status quo,
arguing against the injustices of the day.*

*In Islam, Abraham is revered as a father figure
for all the prophets, and when I think further
about the prophets, it occurs to me that so
many of them were mavericks. They were always
upsetting the proverbial apple cart. Moses
challenged Pharaoh by setting free the slaves.
Joseph was falsely imprisoned by the ruler but
was then released to save Egypt. Jesus upturned*

the money-changers' tables and generally made a
nuisance of himself to the Romans.

When I skip ahead to the current era, so many
of the people I admire were thorns in the side
of the Establishment. Gandhi was very irritating
to the British Empire with all his non-violent
resistance. Mandela was a real pain in refusing
to accept apartheid. Even little Rosa Parks
ruffled feathers by simply refusing to sit at
the back of a bus. But it is not just social
revolutionaries — think of designers, of artists,
of scientists. All question our acceptance of
present reality as the only reality.

People often think of religion as limiting.
For me, the people who are marked down as the
religious greats were often the biggest mavericks
in humanity's history. They cared enough about
the Earth and their fellow humans to attempt to
change the world. It was not gratuitous rebellion
but rather a genuine concern to create a better
reality. Even though the world wears me down
at times, I do believe that ultimately we have
the capacity to change things, and we should
relentlessly pursue a better future for all.

RACHEL MANN

POET, THEOLOGIAN AND PRIEST-IN-CHARGE OF THE CHURCH OF ST NICHOLAS, BURNAGE

Broadcast 00:45 | 2 September 2015

This week I learned a new word: 'pseudocide'. It refers to the act of faking your own death in order to give yourself a fresh start. The most famous fictional example is that fantastic comedy character created by David Nobbs and played brilliantly by Leonard Rossiter: Reginald Perrin, who faked his death to escape his boring, suburban, office life. I'm sure most of us have wished we could start over just to relieve the often tiresome burdens of life.

I SPEAK AS SOMEONE WHO DID START OVER.

I'm a trans woman, and in the early 1990s I transitioned from male to female. I was trying to be more authentically me; it was not so much that I was running away from something as trying

to become a more complete human being. Although I found the process emotionally and socially costly, it was a fresh start in the profoundest sense — a discovery of who I really was.

It was also a reminder that being human is not like being a snake that sheds its skin and becomes completely new. Jesus talks about how, through God, we can be 'born again' — that the Spirit of God can give us our true selves.

MY EXPERIENCE SUGGESTS THAT BEING BORN AGAIN IS A REWEAVING OF THE VARIOUS THREADS OF OUR LIVES.

As an old prayer says, in God nothing is ever truly lost. God is all about fresh starts. But if those fresh starts are to be authentic, they must always respect our past.

4

'ARE OUR HEARTS CLOSE enough TO HEAR GOD'S DIVINE whispers?'

Bilal Hassam

BILAL HASSAM

CREATIVE DIRECTOR AT BRITISH MUSLIM TV

Broadcast 00:45 | 26 April 2015

*It is often said that what distinguishes human
beings from their fellow creatures is their
remarkable methods of communication. I remember
reading a story about a wise man who asked his
students: 'Why do we shout when we're angry? Even
if the other person is sat right next to us?' The
students discussed this amongst themselves, but
the question perplexed them. Finally, the teacher
explained, saying: 'When two people are angry,
their hearts are far apart. To cover all that
distance they have to shout to be able to hear
each other. The angrier they get, the louder they
shout to overcome all that distance.'*

*The teacher continued: 'When two people are in
love, they don't need to shout and they talk to
each other gently. That is because their hearts
are close and the distance between them is
small.' He finished with one last enquiry: 'What
happens, then, when they fall deeper in love?*

Well, then a whisper is enough and, as they get closer to each other, their hearts fall deeper in love until finally they need not even whisper, for then their hearts are intertwined and that is all they ever need.'

It's a beautiful story about communication, and it got me thinking about how people of faith communicate with God. Should we shout and wail about our problems or are our hearts close enough to hear His divine whispers? For centuries Muslim scholars have debated about the best name with which to call upon God, but perhaps they've missed the point. 'What's in a name?' Shakespeare's Juliet asks. 'That which we call a rose by any other name would smell as sweet.' The name, whether you say 'God', 'Allah' or 'Dios', is merely the door that opens into the One, the infinite Divine Source. Perhaps the greatest name is the one that need not even be whispered but emanates instead from a sincere heart. As Muslim scholar and mystic Ibn Ata Allah wrote: 'There is no real distance between you and God in order for you to journey. And the connection between you and God is not cut such that you need to mend it.'

EPHRAIM MIRVIS

CHIEF RABBI OF THE UNITED HEBREW CONGREGATIONS OF THE COMMONWEALTH

Broadcast 09:20 | 27 November 2013

One of my favourite songs is 'Who Am I?' from Les Misérables. For the ex-convict Jean Valjean, the song is a question of personal identity. His answer, '24601', reflects the limitations that others have placed upon him. Like most people, when I first meet somebody, my instinct is to find a personal connection. So, who am I? I am a husband, son, brother, father and grandfather. I was born in South Africa. I have lived in Israel, Ireland and now the United Kingdom. I am Jewish and I support Tottenham Hotspur. These multiple aspects of my identity provide a basis on which to find common ground with others and to begin to establish meaningful connections.

Tonight, we Jewish people around the world will light a candle for the first night of Chanukah, which celebrates identity and belonging. In doing so, we will remember how, nearly 2,200 years

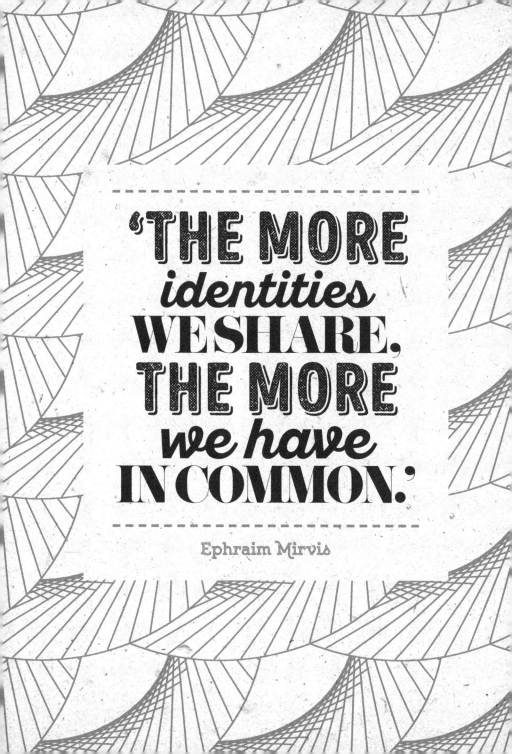

'THE MORE *identities* WE SHARE, THE MORE *we have* IN COMMON.'

Ephraim Mirvis

ago, the Greek Empire sought to force the Jews of ancient Israel to give up their faith and long-held traditions. In a small outpost in the Holy Land, a band of Jews led by Judah Maccabee wrote themselves into history by defeating the Greek armies — at least temporarily. Greater than their military defeat, though, was what they were fighting for: the right to determine their own identity and to give their own answer to the question 'Who am I?'

At Chanukah, we reflect on how we define ourselves and the value of shared identity. Whether as part of a family, a community or a nation, we each have multiple and overlapping identities at our core. This complex tapestry is hugely significant, adding richness and meaning to our lives; and the more identities we share, the more we find we have in common. However, at the same time there is strength in diversity. Attempts to impose one's identity on others is counterproductive. If, as individuals, we can appreciate the equal value of those who share our identity and those who don't, then our combined future will be all the brighter. So, who am I? Just like you, I'm someone who delights in what we share and who takes great pleasure in what makes us unique.

EPHRAIM MIRVIS

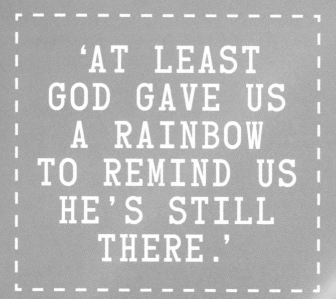

'AT LEAST
GOD GAVE US
A RAINBOW
TO REMIND US
HE'S STILL
THERE.'

Shoshana Boyd
Gelfand

SHOSHANA BOYD GELFAND

DIRECTOR OF JHUB, A JEWISH CHARITY SUPPORTING SOCIAL CHANGE

Broadcast 05:45 | 13 November 2013

A few days ago, I came home to find my six-year-old son sorting through his toys. When I asked what he was doing, he told me that he needed to send some of them to the Philippines to the children whose toys were carried away in the flood. We talked about the terrible storm in the Philippines and what else we could do to help. Then came the question I was dreading: 'Mummy, why didn't God just send an ark the way he did with Noah?'

I didn't know what to say. For my son, this biblical story had suddenly taken on a new dimension. It was no longer the upbeat Sunday-school song about animals marching in two by two. Instead, it was a profound question about why God allows natural disasters to happen and why people suffer in the world.

I had no answer for my son. But in one of my
rare, inspired 'mummy moments', I turned the
question back on him: 'I don't know, sweetheart
— what do you think?' From the mouth of a babe,
he provided me with the only possible answer: 'I
don't know either, Mummy. But at least God gave
us a rainbow to remind us He's still there.'

My son is right. The Noah's Ark story ends
with a rainbow; a promise that the world will
never be completely destroyed again. The Jewish
blessing that is recited upon seeing a rainbow
is zocher ha-brit, which translates as 'reminder
of the covenant'. As difficult as it is for
me to recite this blessing in the face of the
devastation in the Philippines, it is a reminder
that no matter how bad things are and how much
destruction surrounds us, the world will go on
and God has not completely abandoned us.

There may be no ark to save the people of the
Philippines, but we will send aid and support
— and toys. And, hopefully, the people of the
Philippines will know that not only does God
remember them, but we do, too.

YY RUBINSTEIN
ORTHODOX RABBI, AUTHOR AND SPEAKER

Broadcast 00:45 | 24 January 2014

Jews are required to gather together to pray three times a day: in the morning, in the afternoon and at night-time. Every morning at my little synagogue, I see the same old fellow hobbling along holding onto a 'walker', which helps him overcome the fact that his right leg doesn't work very well. Don't try and help him climb the four stairs into the building.

He wants to climb those steps himself.

Every morning at prayer service, this old fellow, who is called Moshe, buries himself in his prayer book and begins his daily conversation with God. He prays for his children and grandchildren and, I suspect, has a word or two with the Almighty about his uncooperative right leg. But there is something else about Moshe. Despite his advanced years and his crippled leg, there is his smile.

He is never too busy speaking to God that he won't notice a stranger who has turned up to join the prayers. Moshe gets up and limps over to welcome them and take them to a seat. His smile is always there, and it's the first thing that people see when arriving at the synagogue. When one of the little boys goes round collecting donations for charity, Moshe always congratulates him on the good job he has done, which is forever accompanied by his famous smile, causing the little boy holding the charity box to also break into a smile.

In every synagogue there is always a light that burns, recalling the candelabra that shone in the Temple in Jerusalem before it was destroyed 2,000 years ago. But a smile that can welcome a stranger or encourage a little boy to perform a simple task shines much brighter than that light. And when it comes from someone who has to overcome pain and struggle to get to morning prayers, it lights up the entire synagogue.

Smiles are infectious — and we should all try to infect as many people as possible with them.

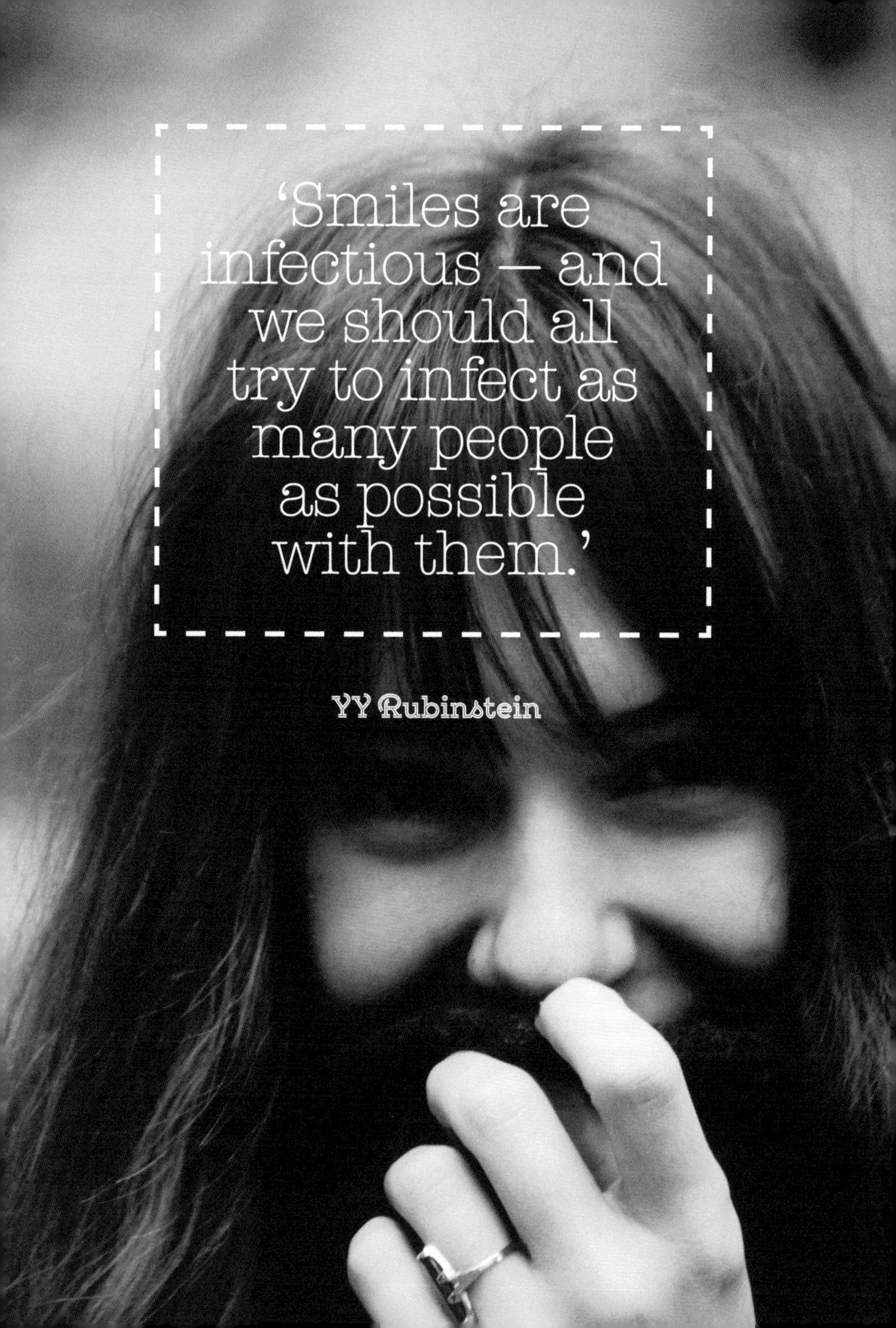

‘Smiles are infectious — and we should all try to infect as many people as possible with them.’

YY Rubinstein

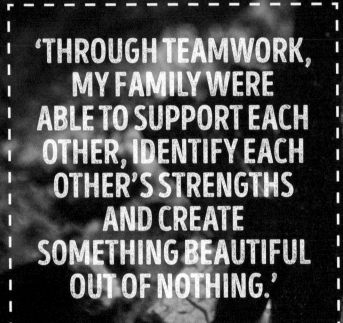

'THROUGH TEAMWORK,
MY FAMILY WERE
ABLE TO SUPPORT EACH
OTHER, IDENTIFY EACH
OTHER'S STRENGTHS
AND CREATE
SOMETHING BEAUTIFUL
OUT OF NOTHING.'

Shaista Aziz

SHAISTA AZIZ
JOURNALIST AND COMEDIAN

Broadcast 00:45 | 30 February 2014

I was seven years old when my grandmother came over from Pakistan to stay with my family in Oxford. Many of the children at school spoke often about their grandparents, but until then I'd never met mine. My grandmother was a mystery to me and I was eager to meet her.

When she finally arrived in England, I was super excited. I remember her being much smaller than I thought — she was fragile and petite with a kind face and a soft velvet voice. So she would feel more at home, my mum and aunts decided to build a tandoor, *a traditional clay oven, to cook* tandoori roti *and evoke memories of village life in Kashmir.*

It still makes me smile to think about the ingenious plan my mum and aunts hatched in order to build the clay oven. They were a group of immigrant women still finding their feet in their

new homeland, but my aunt soon found a builder
who was knocking out the chimney of a house he
was working on. Together with my mother and
another aunt, my aunt rolled the chimney down the
road to her house. Then the three women brought
a steel dustbin and asked the builder to cut a
hole at the front. They lifted the chimney and
cemented it to the dustbin.

Voilà! Through determination and teamwork, a
tandoor was built. In the summer evenings we
would sit with my gran in my aunt's garden as my
mum and aunts worked like a relay team, kneading
the dough to make tandoori roti.

I still remember the delicious taste.

Through teamwork, my family were able to support
each other, identify each other's strengths and
create something beautiful out of nothing.

KATE BOTTLEY
VICAR OF THE CHURCHES OF BLYTH, SCROOBY AND RANSKILL

Broadcast 09:20 | 16 February 2016

I visit the hospital so often, I sometimes think
I should get a loyalty card for the car park.
The other week I found myself going to visit
Maureen, a stalwart member of village life for
the last seven decades, as well as my verger,
church keyholder and friend. Sadly, Maureen knew
she was 'coming in to land', as she put it, and
wanted a chance to chat. As I walked to the lift,
I heard a cry of 'Reverend Kate!' I turned to see
a face I recognised: a young man whose wedding
I'd officiated at just a year or two ago. 'It's
a girl!' he shouted, 'Come and meet her!' I was
taken in to see the lovely Lucy, just an hour old
and fast asleep in the arms of her glowing but
exhausted mother. 'Would you bless her?' the new
father asked. With nothing else to hand, I looked
around and saw a bottle of Prosecco open on the
nightstand. I marked little Lucy with the sign of
the cross and had a quick sip myself.

Then I went up to Maureen's floor. I sat and read the Psalms to her, we prayed and she told me off for turning down the volume on the telly. And I blessed her with the sign of the cross just as I had done with little Lucy, and we said goodbye. A life well lived.

Now, you might think that only one of those hospital beds was a joyful place when I visited that evening. Not so. Little Lucy's mum and dad were excited to welcome the next stage of their lives and, in a strange sort of way, so was Maureen. As she put it: 'I love Jesus and I should very much like to go and meet him, if that's all the same to you.'

At marvellous Maureen's goodbye service I told stories of her life, and in the many years ahead I look forward to seeing what lovely Lucy gets up to. Because it's not the manner of our birth or death that really matters. What really defines us is the bit in the middle and how we make the most of the time we have. Farewell, Maureen, and welcome to the world, little Lucy. I know you both have awfully big adventures ahead.

'Farewell, Maureen, and welcome to the world, little Lucy. I know you both have awfully big adventures ahead.'

Kate Bottley

'THEY LEARN TO see beyond ILLNESS, AGE AND PHYSICAL deformity to THE CHARACTER AND SPIRIT OF the person THEY ARE caring for.'

Cardinal Vincent Nichols

CARDINAL VINCENT NICHOLS

ARCHBISHOP OF WESTMINSTER

Broadcast 09:20 | 17 July 2014

On Sunday I'm off to Lourdes, the pilgrim shrine
in the Pyrenees. We go at the invitation of
Mary, mother of Jesus, who appeared there to
Bernadette, a poor, sickly child and one of the
town's outcasts. She taught Bernadette how to
pray and place her trust in God. We go to learn
the same lessons.

A thousand people go on the pilgrimage with me,
and we join the millions who attend every year.
Among them are many who are seriously ill and
numerous others with significant special needs.
The journey is tough going, but the pilgrimage
is a highlight of the year and a time of lasting
grace and deep friendship.

In Lourdes the sick are given pride of place.
Traffic gives way to wheelchairs and space is
always made for them in the cafés and bars.

Young volunteers are ready to help. In Lourdes they learn to see beyond the terrible effects of illness, age and physical deformity to the character and spirit of the person they are caring for. Each day they learn to express the compassionate love of God who never abandons us, even when we feel lost ourselves.

Here, all the lessons about caring for the sick and dying are spelled out boldly: the innate dignity of each person; the exhausting demands and the rewards of caring for them; the horizon of eternity and heaven; and how, through love, care and medical skill, we help each other to bear the sufferings that life brings. Here, there is no talk of the futility of needless suffering, or that suffering should have the last word on our existence. There are no cruel implications that the terminally ill are a burden on our way of life and our resources. Here, no one points to the dark door of suicide, whether assisted or not. On our pilgrimage, true perspectives will be restored. We'll come home full of joy in the Lord and in one another. It's a great week, a lesson for life and one I never want to miss!

Connect!

Liverpool

Gary Styles

Nantwich,
Cheshire

Andrew Oakes

New Brighton,
Merseyside

Jayne Jones

Pontypool,
Torfaen

Carol Thomas

Avoriaz, France

Oliver Websdell

Hope Valley,
Derbyshire

Helen Shallow

Photographs taken by **Pause for Thought** listeners of
the of the things that made them stop and think (visit
the **Pause for Thought** homepage for more great images)

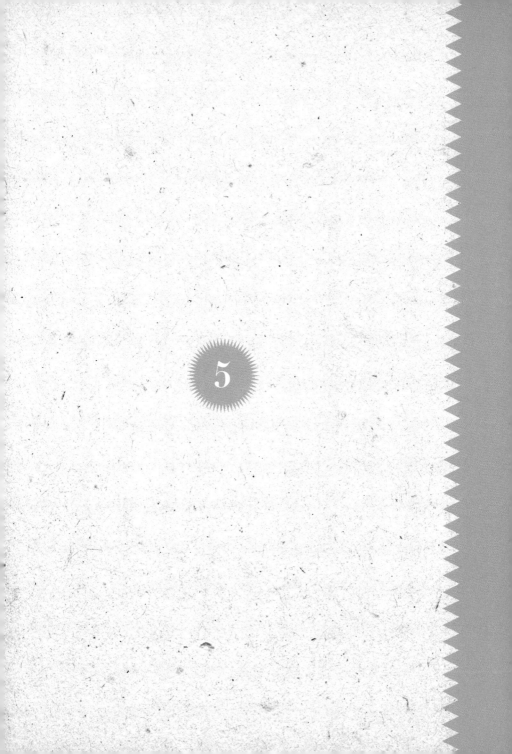

5

'True love is like a thousand rays of light, illuminating our lives and connecting us to the source of all love.'

Abdul-Rehman Malik

ABDUL-REHMAN MALIK

JOURNALIST AND BROADCASTER

Broadcast 09:20 | 13 February 2015

I have to admit that, although I'm all for celebrating love, I have a somewhat ambivalent relationship with Valentine's Day. Growing up, I was never the most popular kid in school and I was certainly no Don Juan when it came to schoolyard entanglements.

Truthfully, I was hesitant and awkward when it came to romance.

In kindergarten, when love was an emotion freely given, you made Valentine's cards for everyone. It was innocent and sweet. But things change as you grow up — the stakes get higher. Sending a Valentine's card starts to mean something different. In high school, if you were lucky, some secret or not-so-secret admirer would slip a note into your locker. In my school, you could send some heart-shaped confectionery to that special someone for a dollar. While some desks would be crowded by peppermint hearts, others remained empty — usually my own.

Whether you are looking desperately for love — as I probably was in those days — or have found it — as I finally did more than 13 years ago — it's easy to get cynical about candlelight dinners, overpriced bouquets and Internet dating. But we all yearn for affection, acceptance and passion.

Sometimes all we want is a love that overwhelms us; that takes us to places we wouldn't have gone otherwise.

The great sages of the Muslim tradition knew about this love. For them, God was the true beloved because God was the source of all love. They spoke of God as an elusive lover and they became mad with desire. 'The minute I heard my first love story, I started looking for you, not knowing how blind that was,' confessed the mystic Rumi. 'Lovers don't finally meet somewhere, they're in each other all along.'

When we see the beauty of a lover, Rumi seems to say, we really see the splendour of God. Even the mystics understood that sometimes passion is a rocky road that leads us into shades of grey — dark, dangerous places, which excite and frighten us.

I wish I'd learned as a kid that true love — the kind that is tested and endures — is something more. It is like a thousand rays of light, illuminating our lives and connecting us to the source of all love. After all, it is the place from which we all came.

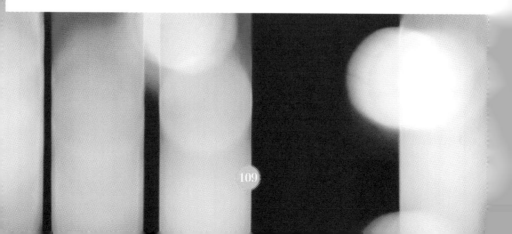

'HOW Can I be THE BEST without BECOMING SELFISH?'

Christopher Jamison

CHRISTOPHER JAMISON
BENEDICTINE MONK

Broadcast 09:20 | 8 September 2014

I was working recently with a group of young
people in their twenties who were on retreat.
'Going on retreat' is when people venture
somewhere quiet, switch off their phones and
engage in dialogue about what matters most in
their lives. This group was old enough to have
done the student bit and they were now asking
themselves the age-old question: 'What do we
really want out of life?' Usually, to 'want'
something means wanting to possess it, whether
that's a car or just a cup of tea.

But these young people wanted more than just to
possess things. They had noticed that there's
another kind of desire that goes deeper than
wanting. They talked about their innermost
longings for love, for goodness and for God.
They were ambitious for what St Paul called
'the higher gifts': faith, hope and love. One
remarked that if this ambition is to be more

than daydreaming, it has to be worked at. Another then asked, 'But how can I be the best without becoming selfish?'

These young people had hit upon something important. Longing for something is not about wanting to possess it. The meaning of 'longing' is found in another word from which it derives: 'belonging' — and to belong is to be loved. The challenge is to make sure that pursuing wants doesn't suffocate these deep longings. I believe wisdom is balancing my wants and my longings, but few of us get that balance right. So I find it a salutary exercise at the end of the day to review how that day's balance went,

asking God to give me the grace to want less and to love more.

As the student said, to be more than a daydream, it has to be worked at ...

JEREMY GORDON
RABBI OF NEW LONDON SYNAGOGUE

Broadcast 09:20 | 21 May 2014

When I met the woman I was to marry, she lived in London and I lived in New York. I hated being in a long-distance relationship; it felt lonely and frustrating. I found the time difference as bad as the physical distance. We'd speak often enough but 7pm in New York was midnight in London and, while I would be feeling bright and breezy, she would be winding down for the night. It was often hard to feel like we were simultaneously present in the same phone conversation.

Feeling down, I went for a coffee with a couple who had also done long distance. They had no answers, but they reminded me of another former long-distance couple who had found a way to make waiting for love work. Then I remembered another couple, and another. It didn't take too long for my then girlfriend and I to join that particular club by celebrating our marriage, now more than a decade ago. Since then I've done more than 150

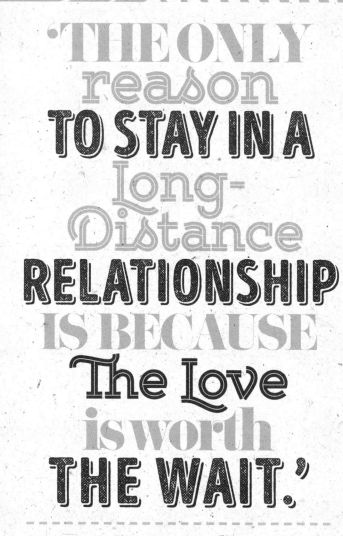

'THE ONLY reason TO STAY IN A Long-Distance RELATIONSHIP IS BECAUSE The Love is worth THE WAIT.'

Jeremy Gordon

weddings as a rabbi, and a surprisingly high number of the couples had previously been in long-distance relationships.

So this is my rabbinic and personal theory on long-distance love. There is only one reason to stay in a long-distance relationship, and that is because the love is worth the wait. There's not much point being unsure and hanging on in there, because the 'hanging around' thing is lonely and frustrating. Pretty soon you have to push for a level of honesty about the relationship that you can delay for a while when your partner lives around the corner.

I'm not sure that absence makes the heart grow fonder, but distance makes a relationship clearer more quickly than proximity. As the French thinker François de La Rochefoucauld wrote: 'Absence diminishes small loves and increases great ones, as the wind blows out the candle and fans the bonfire.'

'MARRIAGE IS ABOUT CARING FOR EACH OTHER WHEN SICK, FRIENDSHIP, LAUGHTER, GOOD TIMES, BAD TIMES AND COMPANIONSHIP TILL DEATH DO US PART ...'

Shazia Mirza

SHAZIA MIRZA

COMEDIAN AND COLUMNIST

Broadcast 05:45 | 15 May 2014

Marriage. That's all my parents talk about. 'Why aren't you married? I have five children and only one of them is married! Where did we go wrong? We will die soon, you should all be married before we go.' They always used to say to me, 'You must marry a Muslim because we are Muslims.' Now they're so desperate, they say, 'Marry anything! We don't mind. As long as he is functioning.' I love the way they lower their standards, beliefs and expectations the more desperate they get.

The reason they go on about marriage so much is because the Qur'an clearly says that in contrast to other religions, such as Christianity and Buddhism, that consider celibacy a means of salvation, Islam sees marriage as one of the most virtuous institutions. The Prophet declared, 'There is no monasticism in Islam ... Whoever is able to marry should marry.' It is considered good for your health, happiness, future and faith. It is the process by which two people who love each other make their relationship public, official and permanent. It is the joining of two people in a bond. They make promises to each other with a view to these lasting a lifetime.

Yes, I'd like to marry George Clooney at the top of the Eiffel Tower, but life is not one long romantic comedy, or so my mother tells me. We all have a romantic perception of love, but I meet people who've been married 40 or 50 years and they're still happy and having fun. It's not about having a handsome husband or a beautiful wife any more or about who cooks dinner and who puts the bins out. It's more about caring for each other when sick, friendship, laughter, good times, bad times and companionship till death do us part. So many things are disposable these days, but most people go into marriage hoping it may be for ever. It requires hard work, but old people tell me it can be wonderful.

I've been to the cinema by myself, I've been on holiday by myself, I've lived by myself. I think I might get married now, this party for one is becoming terribly boring and I really do need someone to put my bins out.

REMONA ALY
JOURNALIST AND MEDIA SPECIALIST

Broadcast 05.45 | 4 December 2015

One of my favourite childhood foods was alphabet spaghetti. I marvelled as the tomato juice oozed between the 'A's and 'L's and 'R's and thought it was a miracle in food engineering. I also loved my mum's Indian dhaal, and downed both these food items to the extent that I'm convinced spaghetti juice and lentil soup are running in my veins.

As with the alphabet spaghetti and dhaal, my generation feels constantly formed — and challenged — by two different worlds. I've lived between first and second generations while navigating a new identity; I've gone from handwriting essays in the 20th century to swiping on my smartphone in the 21st. I also grew up in a pre-9/11 era when things appeared more stable, but I've spent my adult life trying to make sense of a world that seems eager for war. I've seen so much change so quickly. I know that my parents crossed oceans to get here, yet I

'YOU CAN LIGHT A CANDLE OR BE ENGULFED BY THE DARKNESS.'

Remona Aly

also feel big waves of uncertainty. Yet, when I reflect on my life, my generation and my future, I think to myself: it's complicated — but it's still hopeful.

One thing I learned from my parents' generation, who had far less then I do, was their attitude of never giving up. There's an Islamic saying that goes: 'If you have a sapling in your hand, plant it, even if it's the Last Hour.' Nothing says elbow grease to me more than that. The notion of planting a tree while the world is falling around your ears tells me to do everything I can to safeguard my generation, and my future, and to be positive and productive, even if it's all going to pot.

The world is not as rosy as it was when that little girl ate her alphabet spaghetti, but as someone said to me once, you can light a candle or be engulfed by the darkness. I choose to strike that match, and never lose hope that I along with the rest of my generation can change things or be the change they want to see in the world. I just need to plant that sapling, come what may.

'EASTER WEEK IS A REMINDER OF THE NATURE AND POWER OF LOVE.'

Leslie Griffiths

LESLIE GRIFFITHS

METHODIST MINISTER AND LIFE PEER IN THE
HOUSE OF LORDS

Broadcast 09:20 | 31 March 2015

*The Easter period is the week of weeks for
Christians — the time when we remember the last
days, hours and minutes of the life of Jesus. It
was a time full of terrible suffering — not just
physical pain but humiliation and dehumanising
mockery. Yet we look to the events of this week
for hope and inspiration and as a reminder of
the nature and power of love. Year after year
I stand amazed at the capacity of Jesus, dying
in agony, to care for others. He commends those
baying for his blood to God's mercy; he gives
hope to the criminal dying alongside him; he
makes sure that his mother will be cared for
properly once he's dead. 'Look after her,' he
urges his closest friend.*

*The force of this incident came home to me some
years ago when I was chaplain to an adolescent
cancer ward. I remember standing with a teenage*

boy and his distraught mother while a consultant tried to tell them there was nothing more that could be done for him. The doctor stumbled over his words; he just couldn't find the right phrases. It was very embarrassing. Then the boy spoke up. 'It's all right,' he said, 'I know the score; I've had long enough to think about it. I'm not afraid, I'm ready to die, I'll be okay.' And then he took my arm and put it around his mother's shoulders. 'It's my mum I'm worried about,' he said, 'You will look after her when I'm gone, won't you, Vic?' He called me 'Vic', short for Vicar. I nodded in reply.

You don't have to be religious to see the connection between that young man and Jesus on the cross. Both show how love can overcome anything that life throws at us. Jesus died on his cross,

yet love was the winner at the end of the day.

NICK BAINES
BISHOP OF LEEDS

Broadcast 09:20 | 19 December 2014

Call me immature, but ever since I became a
vicar I have had a competition with myself: to
get a Bruce Cockburn lyric into every Christmas
sermon. I have now managed to quote the Canadian
songwriter for 27 years. Why? Well, sometimes the
poetry of someone else shines new light onto what
has become familiar, like Christmas. So, instead
of banging on in prose, I drop in a lyric such
as this: 'Like a stone on the surface of a still
river, driving the ripples on forever, redemption
rips through the surface of time, in the cry of a
tiny babe.'

Brilliant, isn't it? In a world dominated by
power, bigness, violence and competitiveness, it
is the cry of a tiny babe that penetrates the
fog and defies the misery. Or, as someone once
put it, there's no point just shouting at the
darkness — light a candle! A small light can
dispel a lot of murkiness.

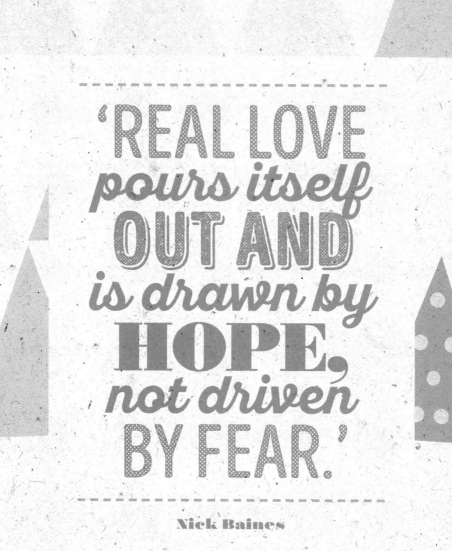

'REAL LOVE pours itself OUT AND is drawn by HOPE, not driven BY FEAR.'

Nick Baines

I think this is how love works — real love. Not some superficial romance, but the committed love that gets stuck into the world as it is and doesn't just wait for it to be as we would like it to be. Real love pours itself out and is drawn by hope, not driven by fear. It seems to me that this is what Christmas is about, really. That God doesn't wait until we have sorted ourselves out, but rather comes into the world as one of us in a way that we can recognise. This, I think, is what real love is about: God committing himself to all the vulnerabilities of human existence happening in a complicated place.

This isn't just the icing on the top of the Christmas cake; it's the sherry-soaked fruit in the heart of it. It's not the peripheral dad-dancing I do to embarrass my kids; it's the strictly committed tango that real dancers do. It isn't some namby-pamby camping 'experience', but the full-blooded live-by-your-wits survival stuff in the jungle. Christmas is God getting down and dirty — where we are. Isn't that brilliant? Redemption rips through the surface of time in the cry of a tiny babe.

NICK BAINES

6

'ST IGNATIUS ASKS GOD TO TEACH *him to give* AND NOT TO COUNT THE COST.'

Ruth Scott

RUTH SCOTT

ANGLICAN PRIEST AND AUTHOR

Broadcast 09:20 | 8 October 2013

At the weekend I bumped into a friend I hadn't seen for a while. Last year her grandson was critically ill and required intensive, long-term hospital care. Her husband was so grateful to the NHS for saving his grandson's life, he wanted to do more than simply send a thank-you card and flowers, and last week he went into hospital to donate one of his own kidneys. He is now recovering at home and, somewhere in London, a woman he doesn't know is alive because of his kidney. I'm blown away by what he's done and why he did it.

In recent times we've heard much about NHS staff who've failed to give patients the care they need. Yet there is a far greater proportion of doctors and nurses, often working under severe stress, who continue to save lives, heal sick patients and support those who are dying on a daily basis. The negative news stories mask their great work, so today I want to honour them. I'm also conscious that, despite the UK being one of the wealthiest nations in the world, too many of us find it too easy to grumble about what we think is going wrong in our society. I sometimes think those who complain the most are the ones who do the least to help put things right, and so I want to honour people like my friend,

whose gratitude leads them to extraordinary acts of generosity.

In one of his famous prayers, St Ignatius of Loyola, the 16th-century saint and founder of the Jesuits, asks God to teach him 'to give and not to count the cost'. St Ignatius's words do not suggest that we shouldn't take seriously the sometimes major personal consequences of what we do for the sake of others. However, they do ask for the courage to pay the price when we see a greater need that can be met. I don't know if I could do what my friend has done, but I find his example profoundly moving, greatly inspiring and deeply challenging.

LALITAVERA

COMMUNITY AND EDUCATION MANAGER OF THE ABBEY THEATRE, DUBLIN

Broadcast 00:45 | 29 November 2013

Every night I try to write down five things I'm grateful for that day.

Sometimes it's hard. I know I should be grateful for food, shelter and family, but some nights my gratitude just feels dutiful — worthy but dishonest — which is annoying because, according to the most lucid moments in my life, I know that this sense of duty is actually more real and a truer response to being alive than the surly resentment I feel when life isn't going my way.

I have no proof except my own experience. But I have to say there have been peak times in my life — out in nature, walking with my children or even once on a Tube platform — when a wider, warmer and less self-absorbed perspective has emerged.

And, irritatingly, one of the lessons of these moments is that the usual way I look at life is limited: limited by fear — of losing control, of not being acknowledged, of not achieving. They are all fears about protecting this thing called a 'self'. Buddhism calls this 'self-cherishing'. It says that what we call a 'self' is really just a useful way of getting by in the world. All the problems start when we think that the self is a fixed, hard, real thing and then strive to protect it.

What gratitude does, whether my ego is feeling it or not at that moment, is to break down the hardness a bit and turn my view outwards to the greater reality that, according to Buddhism and to my own experience, we are all connected. And every time I write down something that I'm thankful for, my ego's power dies a little bit.

It gets a little less hard and I feel a little more connected.

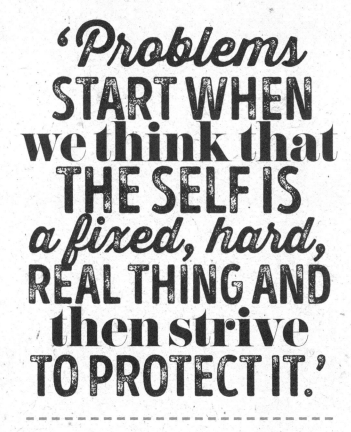

'*Problems* START WHEN we think that THE SELF IS *a fixed, hard,* REAL THING AND *then strive* TO PROTECT IT.'

Lalitavera

MARK TOPPING

VOICEOVER ARTIST AND ACTOR

Broadcast 00:45 | 9 March 2015

Apparently, when my parents were first married,
they offered two Fijian soldiers hospitality
on Christmas Day. Fiji used to be a British
colony, and Methodism is the biggest Christian
denomination there. My parents are also Methodists
and the two who came for Christmas had come over
to England to join the British Army. When it came
to the day, my mum was ill and these soldiers sat
on her sickbed playing guitar and singing Fijian
songs in falsetto. For her, unsurprisingly, a
memorable and strangely enriching experience.

When I was a boy I always wanted our family
gatherings, whether at Christmas or during other
holidays, to be just that — family. No outsiders
— just us, thank you. But most years that I can
remember, there was always someone else there. No
Fijian soldiers, sadly, but always someone. And
every year that this happened, at the end of it
all I thought: You know what? I'm glad they came,

'It's better for all of us if the home is a place of welcome, than if there's an exclusion zone around it.'

Mark Topping

it was more fun. It took me a while to learn that it's better for all of us if the home is a place of welcome, than if there's an exclusion zone around it.

And what I picture, thinking back, is how great the meals together were with these extra guests, the stories and laughter, the 'too much food' and the warm atmosphere. One of the images Jesus uses time and again is of a meal, a banquet, a feast. It features in numerous parables. And, invariably, an essential feature of these 'Kingdom of God get-togethers' that Jesus speaks of is that there are people there you wouldn't expect. In one story the person throwing the feast tells his servants to go out into the streets and bring in all the poor, the sick and the homeless they can find.

If I'd had my way as a child, we would have battened down the hatches and been just us, no strangers. But we'd all have missed out on so much. I don't think God wants anyone to miss out.

According to Jesus, his invitation list is limitless.

SHERIDAN VOYSEY
WRITER AND BROADCASTER

Broadcast 05:45 | 19 March 2015

My wife and I spent Christmas with friends on the Isle of Mull. What an enchanted place that is — the snow-capped mountains, the dramatic skies, the vivid yellows and browns of the landscape. One moment we drove through snowstorms, the next we watched the sun pierce through the clouds and flood the misty valley with amber light. Sitting in the conservatory of our holiday shack, we saw double rainbows from end to end. To me, Mull felt like a place of fairytales.

Natural beauty like that makes me happy. So do long train rides, second-hand bookshops, cosy pubs on rainy days, an engaging conversation, the giggles of a child, the music of New Order and Florence and the Machine, a good dim sum restaurant, crêpes with sugar and lemon, a reader telling me one of my books has helped them, and cherries dipped in dark chocolate. (To paraphrase Benjamin Franklin's famous words,

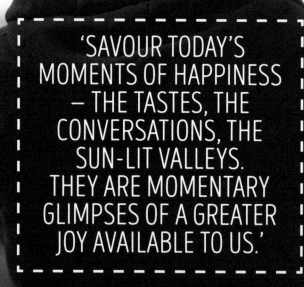

'SAVOUR TODAY'S
MOMENTS OF HAPPINESS
– THE TASTES, THE
CONVERSATIONS, THE
SUN-LIT VALLEYS.
THEY ARE MOMENTARY
GLIMPSES OF A GREATER
JOY AVAILABLE TO US.'

Sheridan Voysey

chocolate is proof enough that God exists and wants us to be happy.)

It has been said that the Bible has more to impart about joy than it does about happiness — and for good reason. All those things that make me happy are momentary. The chocolate-dipped cherries are soon gone. The song is over after three-and-a-half minutes. Mull's rainbows fade as quickly as they appear. In contrast, I believe Christian joy is enduring. It comes from the Spirit of Christ who comes to live within us when we ask him to, and I've found this joy can be experienced even in unhappy times.

But my Bible also tells me that every good and perfect gift is from God, including ephemeral things like sunshine, food and happiness. God made the cherry. God gave humans the ability to make chocolate. The combination of the two is divine, however fleeting the eating experience. So savour today's moments of happiness — the tastes, the conversations, the sun-lit valleys. They are momentary glimpses of a greater joy available to us.

'I love a celebration — especially if I've had to wait for it.'

Malcolm Doney

MALCOLM DONEY

ANGLICAN PRIEST, WRITER AND EDITOR

Broadcast 05:45 | 14 July 2015

*I love a celebration — especially if I've had to
wait for it. For the last week or so, we've been
eating courgettes and strawberries from the garden.
Scrumptious! Of course, we could have been eating
those all year, plucked from supermarket shelves.
But I love the fact that we've had to wait for the
season to come round, watching them become more
plump and glossy each day until, finally, we can
get out there with the old trug and harvest away
— ending up with a plateful of summer. It always
reminds me of that passage in the Hebrew Book of
Ecclesiastes, which was turned into a song by folk
singer Pete Seeger and later made into a hit by The
Byrds. There's 'a time to plant, a time to reap',
it goes. 'A time to weep, and a time to laugh; a
time to mourn, and a time to dance.'*

*For me, celebrations are sweetest when they come
out of a time of testing. They could be as simple
as a welcome pint after a difficult week or a*

decent lie-in after a run of broken sleeps. They
are important tags, a way of saying anything from
'We did it!', to 'Boy, I'm glad that's over!'
Muslims mark Eid – an eruption of feasting that's
been anticipated during 30 days of fasting. For
Christians, the Easter festival rises out of the
sombre days of Lent, and Christmas is born from
the patient waiting of Advent. Life needs its peaks
and troughs. Take the first day of the school
summer holidays. I hated school, so I'd mentally
count down the days of June and July like a jailed
convict until that delicious first day of freedom
dawned. No angry wake-up call from downstairs, no
nasty uniform to get into, no rushed breakfast –
just a day of unfettered liberty yawning open ...

Celebrations – whether they're religious or not –
can still be holy moments. They are like bookmarks
telling us where we've got to. They're an essential
way of recognising that something significant
has been achieved, of saying thank you to friends,
family, teammates, the Divine ... whoever.
Therefore we look one another in the eye, repeat
old stories, raise a glass, celebrate the past and
the present, and look to the future.

JULIA NEUBERGER

SENIOR RABBI TO THE WEST LONDON SYNAGOGUE AND LIFE PEER IN THE HOUSE OF LORDS

Broadcast 09:20 | 27 April 2015

During the depths of winter, I always bring in
the amaryllis bulbs that have been languishing
outside on the windowsill since last year, clean
their pots and give them a bit of water and
fertiliser. Just this last week, they've been
rewarding me with the most spectacular display
of salmon-pink blooms, and they make me smile as
I walk into my kitchen. The bulbs were given to
me some seven or eight years ago, and yet back
they come every year. My flowers give me enormous
pleasure. My children tell me, as I talk to them
about my few gardening successes, 'Mum, you're
just getting old.'

But it's not just an older person's pleasure.
The emphasis on planting gardens goes back to the
Bible. The prophet Jeremiah told the Israelite
exiles in Babylon to 'Build houses and live in

'We should remind ourselves to delight in burgeoning nature, for we need that sense of renewal each year.'

Julia Neuberger

them; plant gardens and eat their produce.' The prophet Isaiah used the metaphor of a vineyard that God had nurtured but which failed to reward its owner with lavish grapes. Faced with only wild, bitter fruit, the owner threatened to uproot the vineyard. King Ahab took Naboth's vineyard and used it as a vegetable garden, even though Naboth had refused to sell it. Gardens are everywhere in the Bible and ancient literature. They're deeply rooted in our way of thinking, whether we're young or old. And at this time of year they make us all smile, with the feeling that everything is going to be plentiful once again.

I think we should remind ourselves to delight in burgeoning nature, for we need that sense of renewal each year. It gives us hope and a cause for gratitude, which we don't acknowledge often enough. My flowering bulbs make me say thank you. And each year, as everything starts flowering once again, I am just grateful to be alive. We could all share that gratitude, and perhaps even show it, by gardening more, giving each other more plants and celebrating life.

JULIA NEUBERGER

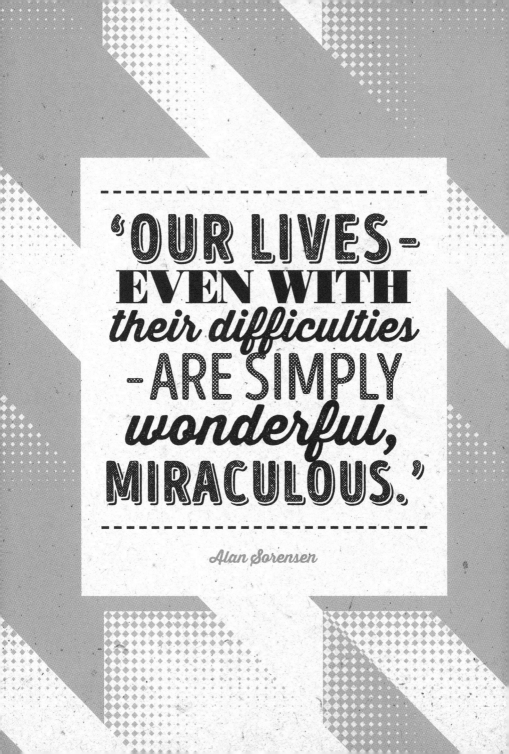

ALAN SORENSEN
CHURCH OF SCOTLAND MINISTER

Broadcast 05:45 | 29 November 2013

Anyone who says the UK doesn't do Thanksgiving clearly didn't notice the mass celebrations in its streets in recent days — the nation falling to its knees to offer prayers of joy and gratitude. Okay, it may not have been quite like that, but an awful lot of people were happy to hear that the Monty Python team was reuniting — so happy that the tickets sold out in an instant. One of their many brilliant sketches etched into my mind and the national consciousness is 'What have the Romans ever done for us?' It starts out as a bitter complaint, but the answers keep coming. 'All right, but apart from sanitation, medicine, education, wine, public order, irrigation, roads, the fresh-water system and public health, what have the Romans ever done for us?' There's a lot to be thankful for.

Now, I often get accused of being a bit of a Pollyanna, always looking on the bright

side of life, and to that accusation I reply,
'Absolutely!' To the question whether the glass
is half-full or half-empty, I usually answer
with something like, 'Wow, we've got a glass with
stuff in it! Isn't that great!' I want to thank
God for all that I see around me. The world is a
fantastic place, and our lives — even with their
difficulties — are simply wonderful, miraculous.
I'm very happy to say 'thanks' till the cows come
home for all the good stuff that comes my way.

The other reason I'm doggedly thankful is that,
a couple of times in my life, I've suffered from
depression. And anyone who has either had that
disease or been around someone who has it knows
just how black the world can look and how empty
the glass can appear. One technique to help
deal with it is to train yourself to continually
catch the negative thoughts and move your mind
to something positive. In time this can help the
healing process. Being thankful and positive can
apparently alter the mind. So even at a purely
chemical level, thanking God in our prayers is a
healthy thing to do. Just as I put my woollies on
to avoid catching cold, I like to be as thankful
as I can to stay healthy in heart and mind.

Be thankful!

Twywell,
Northamptonshire

Ellie Edwards

Radstock,
Somerset

Steve Hopton

Chesterfield,
Derbyshire

Rachel Pollard

Dunwich, Suffolk

Karen Dutton

Loftus, North
Yorkshire

Jeff Smith

Pinchbeck,
Lincolnshire

Ewa Mackeonis

Photographs taken by *Pause for Thought* listeners of some of the things that made them stop and think (visit the *Pause for Thought* homepage for more great images)

7

'Letting go
OFFERS A
JOURNEY
TO A MORE
mature
RELATIONSHIP.'

GARTH HEWITT

GARTH HEWITT
MUSICIAN AND FOUNDER OF THE
AMOS TRUST

Broadcast 00:45 | 9 June 2014

I can remember a time when Father's Day didn't really exist. Then it gradually began to creep in, and I recall being surprised when my children first presented me with gifts while saying 'Happy Father's Day!'

Up until recently, we were very fortunate in that we had two of our four children living close to us in London, and Saturdays often consisted of brunch together at Broadway Market on the border of Hackney and Bethnal Green. We did many things together. Now one lives in Rio in Brazil and the other lives in Nashville in the States ... another's been in South Africa for years. So three out of four now live abroad.

I'm proud of what all my children are doing, but I'm sorry it has taken them so far away. A poem by Cecil Day-Lewis about a father—son relationship ends by saying that 'selfhood begins with a walking away / And love is proved in the letting go.' In one sense there has been a letting go, although it's hard to say whether I've truly let go or whether they've simply moved away. But in another way, neither side has really had to let go, as we are fortunate to live in times when communication is very easy and cheap. Although a sense of selfhood may begin with the act of walking away and love be proved in the letting go, the process actually offers a journey to a more mature relationship; a relationship where the dynamics change.

THE RELATIONSHIP HAS NOT GONE BUT DEVELOPED, AND IT IS CHERISHED IN NEW, PERHAPS DEEPER, WAYS.

Therefore, this coming Father's Day, I shall receive messages from around the world — and even the grandchildren will join in. Something new and wonderful has opened up — in one way I've had to let go but, in another way, I receive far more back.

RACHEL PARKINSON

MINISTER OF BIRSTALL METHODIST CHURCH

Broadcast 00:45 | 8 April 2015

As a teenager, I practised a way of walking which involved keeping my head down and looking at the ground as far as possible while trying not to bump into lampposts. It was the way our neighbour's daughter walked. She was a couple of years older than me and I thought she looked incredibly sophisticated and aloof. I don't need to tell you that I didn't.

That was just one of the times when I've tried to change myself by copying other people I admire. The results have normally been like one of Cinderella's ugly sisters trying on the glass slipper — try as I might, the shoe simply hasn't fitted, because it isn't mine. A great benefit of middle age is that I have stopped being my own self-improvement project. Don't get me wrong — I'm far from perfect. I'm often brought up short by my own insecurities, I trip over my prejudice and stub my toe on my pride.

'I PICTURE MYSELF AS A SMALL STONE AT THE BOTTOM OF A RIVER. AS I RUB UP ALONG OTHER STONES, I SHAPE THEM AND THEY SHAPE ME.'

RACHEL PARKINSON

But now I don't believe that I am the best person to judge the change that I need, nor do I think I'm the one to bring it about. As judge I now look to the God who made me and who knows both my shortcomings and my potential. And I also know that the major agents of change are the people with whom I share my life.

I picture myself as a small stone at the bottom of a river. As I rub up along other stones, I shape them and they shape me. The more stones that are around me — each of them a different shape and composition — the more my sharp corners are rubbed off. And all these stones rest underneath the current of the river — my metaphor for God. The river shapes us all, although some stones prove more resistant than others. Occasionally, turbulence in the current lifts me up and moves me along to sit with new neighbours, and the reshaping process begins once again.

MUCH BETTER A SMALL STONE IN A RIVER THAN AN UGLY SISTER IN AN ILL-FITTING SHOE.

RACHEL PARKINSON

'IT'S NOT WHAT
HAPPENS TO US
THAT DEFINES
US, BUT HOW
WE REACT.'

JONATHAN HUGHES

JONATHAN HUGHES

RABBI OF THE RADLETT UNITED SYNAGOGUE

Broadcast 05:45 | 3 February 2016

There's a story about a middle-aged man called
David who was going through tough times. He'd
lost his money during the economic crash, his
wife had left him for someone else and his kids
weren't in touch with him. Things were at an
all-time low and he was beginning to lose the
plot. Now, David had never been that religious
but, out of desperation, he decided to go and see
his rabbi. They sat down and David offloaded the
entire sorry tale. But instead of presenting him
with pearls of wisdom, the elderly sage asked
him to boil three pots of water on his stove
and place a potato in one, an egg in another and
some coffee beans in the third. Well, David now
reckoned the rabbi must have more problems than
he did. Perhaps he was simply too deaf to hear
his story and just needed his lunch made for him.
Then, mystifyingly, the rabbi told him to wait
for half an hour while they all boiled away.
David complied out of sheer pity.

Afterwards, the rabbi told him to press down on the potato and the egg with a fork. When he pressed the potato it was so soft it had turned to mush, whereas the egg had turned rock hard. Then they looked at the coffee. Well, it had become a tasty, drinkable pot of coffee!

The rabbi then delivered his advice: 'In life we are placed on a hot stove; onto the fire of life's challenges. When we go through tough times, some people turn to mush like the potato – they are broken. Others become like the egg – so bitter they harden up and lose the ability to love and cherish others. Choose to be like the coffee. It didn't allow its surroundings to diminish it; rather, it transformed its environment.' Teary-eyed, David gave the rabbi a hug and returned to his problems. He began a process that eventually turned his life around.

The rabbi's message is that we shouldn't allow life's heat to defeat us. We have the option to retaliate positively and change the colour of the troublesome waters around us. After all, it's not what happens to us that defines us, but how we react.

DAVE TOMLINSON

WRITER AND VICAR OF ST LUKE'S, HOLLOWAY

Broadcast 05:45 | 14 April 2015

It has been said that the unhappiest people in this world are those who care the most about what other people think. Which confirms my view that the most liberating thing we can experience in life is to find out who we are deep down, and be happy with that regardless of what others think or say.

Far too often our lives are shaped by voices other than our own — by the voices of a parent or teacher, society, popular culture or even religion. Sometimes these voices are legitimate and well intentioned, perhaps very important, but any of them can become our prison if we allow them to. The fact is, it can take a long time to find out who we really are, and even longer to have the courage to become that. After decades of pastoral counselling, I have observed that many of us spend at least half our lives trying to fit in with the expectations of others. Then,

'BE TRUE
TO YOURSELF.
IT MAY
UPSET
OTHERS
(FOR A WHILE).'

DAVE TOMLINSON

eventually, if we do indeed find the courage, we begin to explore the life that we really want to live.

Personal liberation is about being authentic — being true to who we are and what we want deep down. The Hassidic teacher Rabbi Zusha commented wisely that, in the coming world, they will not ask him 'Why were you not Moses?' but rather 'Why were you not Zusha?' One of the best stories of liberation of which I have been a part is that of our lovely daughter Lissy, who took 25 years to come out as being gay. It was like a religious conversion: almost instantly, a weight was lifted from her, and she discovered a completely new level of happiness with herself, with others and with life in general.

'I know you have got lots of gay friends and you're cool about it,' she said, 'but I don't know how you feel about it being one of yours.' Of course, it was lovely that she cared about what we felt, but what really mattered was that she had decided to be true to herself. And, actually, even when she was a child we often said, 'We've got three children: one of each!'

Lissy was always different, and we loved her for it.

LIBERATION AND MEANING EMERGE WHEN WE EACH LIVE OUR OWN LIFE, NOT SOMEONE ELSE'S, AND LIVE IT WITH INTEGRITY.

It's right that we listen to and respect the voices of others (especially those who care for us), but it is more important to discover our own way in life. As Jesus said, 'The truth will set you free.'

Be true to yourself. It may upset others (for a while). It may bring temporary discomfort or embarrassment. But in the end, truth is the path to liberation.

JACQUELINE NICHOLLS

ARTIST AND JEWISH EDUCATOR

Broadcast 09:20 | 17 March 2014

*I'm not sure why it's called retail therapy when
the process of shopping can be so hellish. Going
in and out of various shops, trying on items from
the unsuitable to the ridiculous and negotiating
the variants in sizing, you wonder why you don't
stick with what is already in the wardrobe. And
then you remember what is in your wardrobe — the
tattered, the stained, the out-of-shape stuff —
and so you continue on what is beginning to feel
like an absurd quest. Finally, you find something
that you love — and it fits! Well, there's
nothing like a new item of clothing to make you
feel great. And relieved.*

*There is something exciting about new clothes.
New clothes are enticing, especially when
they're packaged beautifully. They're clean,
pressed, shiny, unworn and unspoiled. Unlike
the items in the wardrobe or crumpled on the
bedroom floor, all the buttons are there, there's*

'**New clothes give us the chance to begin afresh, unblemished and untainted.**'

JACQUELINE NICHOLLS

no sight of a hard-to-shift stain and they haven't become stretched or misshapen. There's no sign of wear and tear — life hasn't touched them yet. New clothes are pristine. Perfect. They can put smiles on our faces on a grey day. It seems faintly ridiculous to say that they make us happy, but they do, and not for superficial reasons. A friend told me that she likes seeing herself in new clothes because, for a split second, she doesn't really recognise herself — she sees someone else. New clothes offer us a promise.

In the Jewish tradition, it is the custom to say a blessing when wearing new, special clothes for the first time. It acknowledges that this marks the beginning of a new chapter in our lives. From then on, we don't have to be the person who spilt food or rushed in the morning and got toothpaste everywhere. We are not worn out. New clothes give us the chance to begin afresh, unblemished and untainted. We are momentarily pristine and perfect. We are ready to face a new day.

'WE ALL HAVE TO come to terms WITH DEATH one way or ANOTHER.'

ANN EASTER

ANN EASTER

CHAPLAIN TO THE QUEEN

Broadcast 09:20 | 18 August 2015

*My dad had been ill for nearly a year when
his condition deteriorated and he was admitted
to hospital. The next morning, on 18 August
– 17 years ago today – the phone rang and a
nurse said to me: 'Your father is significantly
unresponsive.' I told the nurse I'd go to
the hospital immediately. As I put the phone
down, I said to my husband and children: 'It
was the nurse at the hospital. She says Dad's
"significantly unresponsive" ... I think she
means he's died,' and with that, my family and
I started to laugh in that hysterical way that
sometimes happens at times of extreme stress. We
were soon hooting with laughter at the phrase
'significantly unresponsive', because my dad,
who loved words and the way people used them,
would have laughed like a drain at such a coy
euphemism. Then we started thinking of all the
other things she might have said instead, each
of them seeming more hilarious than the last –*

'fallen off his perch', 'given up the ghost',
'popped his clogs', 'kicked the bucket', 'been
called to higher service', 'copped it', 'brown
bread!', 'obiit' — if you're into Latin. At least
she didn't say that my dad had 'failed to fulfil
his wellness potential', a phrase I saw suggested
in a recent medical manual!

We know, of course, why the nurse cloaked the
news — rather than presenting the bald facts, she
used an expression that she hoped might ease the
pain a little. But I always feel that people of
faith can be bold when they talk about death. We
still miss my dad every day — of course we do —
but, as Christians, we believe that his death was
the gateway to a new and golden life in heaven
where he's well, whole and free, and reunited
with my mum and all those friends who went on
before him (and there's another euphemism!).

Dress it up or tell it plain, we all have to come
to terms with death one way or another. The hope
of a life hereafter and the joy of happy memories
do not serve to obscure or shelter us from death,
but rather put it into perspective.

STEVE CHALKE

BAPTIST MINISTER AND FOUNDER OF OASIS UK

Broadcast 00:45 | 4 September 2015

*I once met a man whose life had fallen apart.
A series of rash, short-sighted decisions had
robbed him of his wife and children and had left
him abandoned, alone and jobless. Eventually,
in desperation, he decided to visit the local
bishop's palace to ask for help. He was shown in
and was asked to wait. Minutes later the bishop
appeared and asked how he could help.*

*The man poured out his sorry tale — one filled
with hopelessness, guilt and despair. Having
listened for a while, the bishop suggested to the
man that he sit and reflect on his copy of the
famous oil painting by Rembrandt,* The Return of
the Prodigal Son, *which depicts the homecoming of
the wayward son as recounted in Jesus's parable.*

*Over the next hour, the man just sat gazing at
the Dutch Master's painting. At its very centre
are the hands of the father wrapped around his*

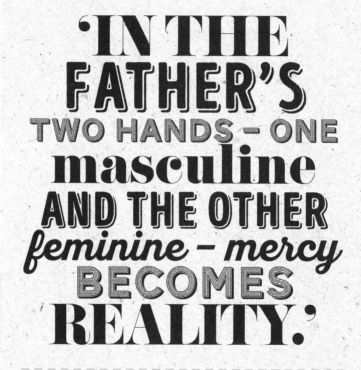

'IN THE FATHER'S TWO HANDS - ONE masculine AND THE OTHER feminine - mercy BECOMES REALITY.'

STEVE CHALKE

wayward and regretful son. But the two hands are painted quite differently. The father's left hand is strong and muscular. It holds the son firmly. It will not let go. But the right hand is different — it caresses the son's shoulder tenderly. It is gentle. It strokes. It's a mother's hand. In the father's two hands — one masculine and the other feminine — mercy becomes reality, and forgiveness, reconciliation and healing are achieved.

The man told me that it was as though the scales fell from his eyes. For the first time in years, God's healing, tender and forgiving presence seemed tangible to him. He relaxed. He was at peace. He felt forgiven by a loving God; he even felt that he was able to forgive himself.

NO LONGER DID HE FEEL TRAPPED BY HIS PAST. HE COULD SEE A NEW CHAPTER AND NEW HOPE.

He broke down in tears — tears of regret, relief and homecoming.

INDEX OF CONTRIBUTORS